All rights reserved. No part of this publication may be reproduced, stored in a retrieval system or transmitted in any form or by any means, whether by electronic, mechanical, photocopying, recording or by other method without the prior permission of the publishers and the copyright holder.

First published 2014
Text copyright Hugo White,
Photographs copyright as noted on picture or acknowledgements.
Cover design and cover photograph SCSTyrrell
Artwork copyright 2013 SCSTyrrell & Pasticcio
Set in Candara 12 on 14.4
Published by Pasticcio Ltd. Registered in England No 5125728
01326 340153   www.pasticcio.co.uk
ISBN 978-0-9570311-5-9

The Great War for Civilization: 1914-1919

An Introduction

Hugo White

Acknowledgements

This introduction to the History of the First World War would not have been possible without the help of many to whom I am grateful for information, photographs and opinions.
Special thanks are due to the staff of the Regimental Museum of the Duke of Cornwall's Light Infantry who have always been supportive and helpful.

Illustration Credits

Many of the photographs were provided by the Trustees of the Duke of Cornwall's Light Infantry's Museum, who are thanked for giving permission for their use.
Illustrations made available by the White family are used with their permission.
Certain illustrations which are said to be within the public domain, and therefore available for reproduction, have been taken from photographic libraries and other sources.
We have tried to trace the origin and owners of illustrations, crediting the owners where possible, or requested. We apologise for omissions or inaccuracies. Where requested, the origin of a particular picture has been noted alongside the illustration.

Maps used include:

The maps on pages 8 and 73: Philips Historical Atlas. George Philip & Son, Ltd, London 1934
Hand drawn maps by Hugo White.

Contents

	Introduction	7
1.	Causes of the War	9
2.	The Conduct of the War	13
3.	The British Forces	15

    The Regular Army, The Territorial Force
    Kitchener's Army, The Conscript Army
    The Fighting Arms: Artillery, Cavalry, Infantry
    The Royal Navy
    Britain's Air Arm

4.	Phases of the War	29
5.	Generalship	47
6.	The Staff	50
7.	Destructive Weapons	52
8.	Living Conditions in the Front Line	56
9.	Campaigns outside Europe	62

    Palestine, Mesopotamia, Salonika, Gallipoli, Africa

10.	Medical History	74
11.	Executions	77
12.	Religion	79
13.	The Armistice	80
14.	The Treaty of Versailles	84
15.	Conclusion	87

    Casualties; Social Change

	Appendix 1: Chart and introduction to the organisation of the British Army.	94
	Appendix 2: Glossary and Biographies	99
	Bibliography	108

Introduction

All history is to some extent subjective but none more so than that of the Great War. An Armageddon of such appalling ferocity was not an event that could, at least initially, be chronicled with dispassion unclouded by emotion. Over the years the pendulum of opinion has swung across a broader arc than at any other similar period in our nation's history, and accounts written in 1919 and 1990 often present such diametrically opposed views that one could be forgiven for failing to realise that they refer to the same events.

This swing of the pendulum has fostered myths which have become enshrined as factual history, and these in turn have been accepted, not only by the general public, but by the survivors of the actual events, who have substituted them in place of their own fading memories. Eye witness accounts of old men are now strongly influenced by both hindsight and mythology; with the very greatest respect to these veterans, their accounts, which should constitute the best primary historical sources, are seldom completely reliable.

Another interesting aspect of these accounts is that, unlike previous conflicts, a small but extremely significant number of intellectual writers and poets served at the front. They were deeply affected by their traumatic experiences and subsequently produced a body of literature unsurpassed in the history of war. There is absolutely no doubt about either the honesty or the personal bravery of these men but it must be emphasised that they were not typical of the great anonymous mass of British soldiers who accepted their appalling duty with robust equanimity, and faced death and mutilation with such phlegmatic valour.

I therefore make no apology for the fact that what follows is my own personal view. It is backed up by considerable reading but, for all that, is undoubtedly controversial. I do not ask you to agree with what I say. However, if it makes you think about one of the greatest tragedies in history, I will have succeeded in my aim.

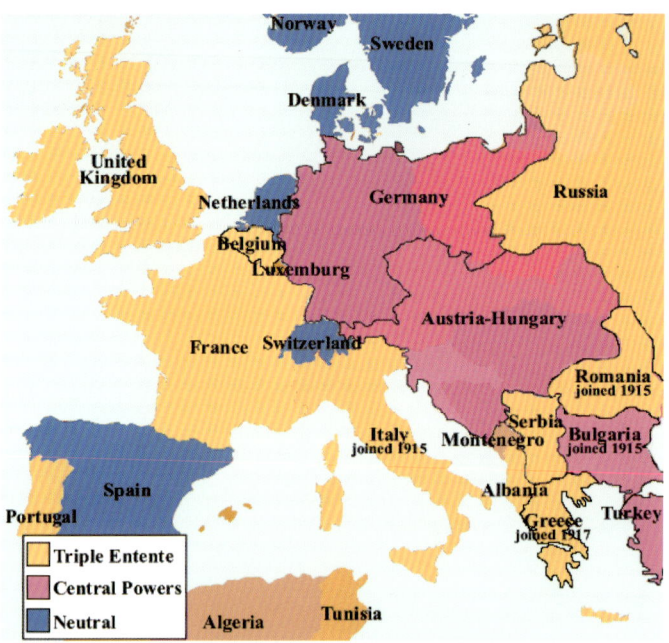

The participants in the First World War.

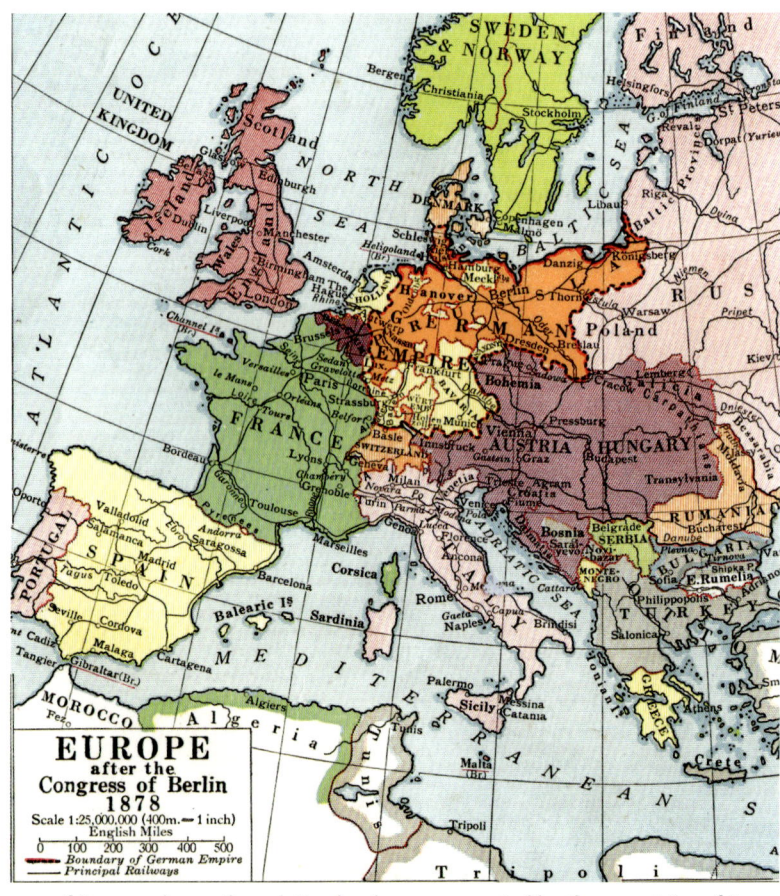

A map of Europe shows the relative land areas occupied by the countries of Europe, before the First World War. *(Map courtesy Philips of London)*

1: Causes of the War

Why the nations of Western Europe, standing at the peak of a civilisation and apparently enjoying a degree of stability never experienced before or since, should have launched themselves into an Armageddon of self destruction will probably never be adequately explained. There were certainly deep undercurrents beneath the superficially smooth surface and many theories have been put forward in an attempt to demonstrate the true causes. These are all subjects for intriguing debate; however, before delving into the mists of speculation, one must understand the actual events which led up to war.

The area known as Belgium had suffered a violent history over the previous two centuries. Armies had moved across its plains and many battles had been fought. After the defeat of Napoleon, the Congress of Vienna had agreed to take the Country out of French control and reinstate it as part of the Netherlands. The Catholic Belgians deeply resented being attached to an extreme Protestant power, and in 1830 rose up under arms against their new masters. While the Dutch attempted to quell the revolt, the French looked on with eager eyes, intent on reclaiming Belgium should the opportunity arise. At that stage, Lord Palmerston stepped in. He realised that if major conflict was to be avoided, Belgium must be set up as a neutral sovereign state. For nine years he negotiated, cajoled and argued with the contenders. On occasions he deployed the might of the Royal Navy to demonstrate his determination. He won the battle. In 1839 a treaty was signed by Great Britain, France, Russia, Prussia and Austria guaranteeing Belgium as an ' independent and perpetually neutral state.'

In the early years of the 20th Century, a grumbling enmity still existed between France and Germany dating back to the Franco-Prussian war of 1870. France had since constructed a massive chain of fortresses across her front, but was flanked by two neutral and undefended countries - Belgium and Switzerland. Switzerland was virtually impassible to an army; Belgium, however, offered the ideal terrain for an outflanking movement. At about this time, Count von Schlieffen, the German Chief of Staff, formulated his famous plan to conquer France by carrying out a great outflanking hook through Belgium before turning south, capturing the Channel ports and cutting off Paris and the French army from the rear. Thus one of the signatories of the 1839 Treaty which had guaranteed the neutrality of Belgium,

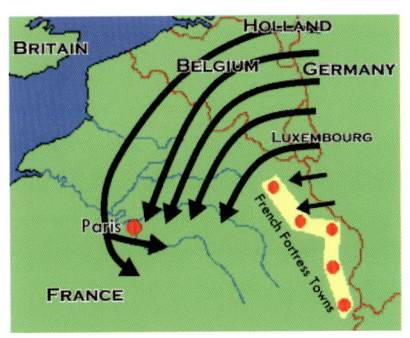

A diagram of the von Schlieffen plan to outflank French defences.

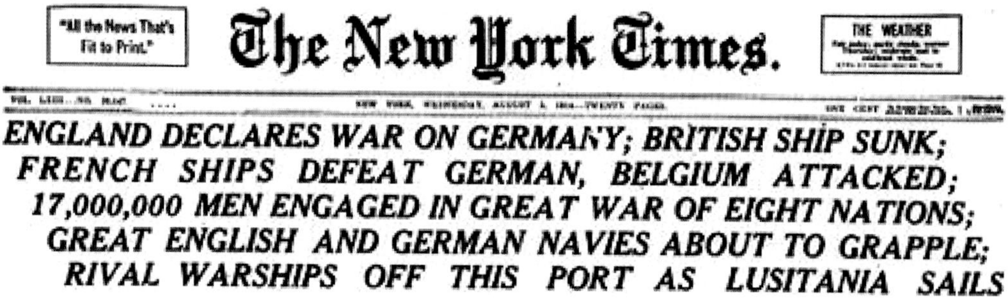

"All the News That's Fit to Print."

The New York Times.

THE WEATHER

ENGLAND DECLARES WAR ON GERMANY; BRITISH SHIP SUNK; FRENCH SHIPS DEFEAT GERMAN, BELGIUM ATTACKED; 17,000,000 MEN ENGAGED IN GREAT WAR OF EIGHT NATIONS; GREAT ENGLISH AND GERMAN NAVIES ABOUT TO GRAPPLE; RIVAL WARSHIPS OFF THIS PORT AS LUSITANIA SAILS

Der Deutsche Correspondent.

Deutschland erklärt England den Krieg.

Ist im Kriegszustand mit Frankreich.

Weltkrieg im vollen Gange.

Deutschland und Oesterreich allein.

Kaiser Wilhelm's bedeutsame Thronrede.

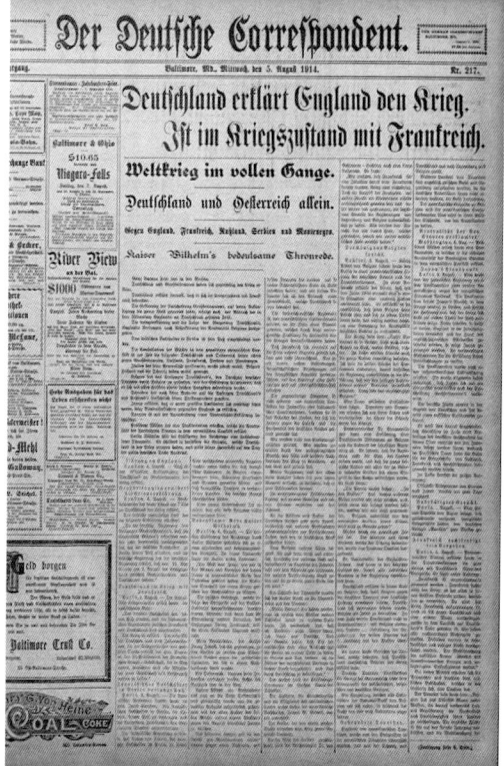

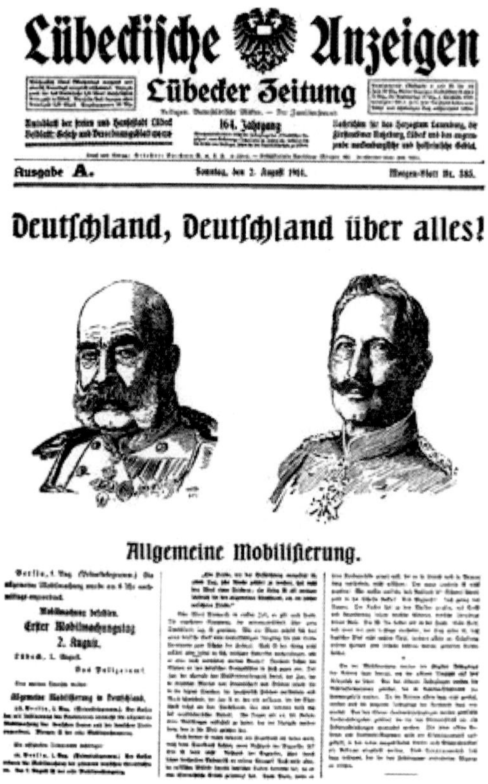

Lübeckische Anzeigen

Lübecker Zeitung

164. Jahrgang

Ausgabe A.

Deutschland, Deutschland über alles!

Allgemeine Mobilisierung.

Mobilmachung befohlen.

Erster Mobilmachungstag 2. August.

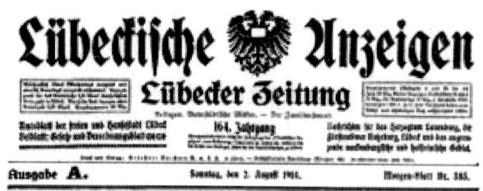

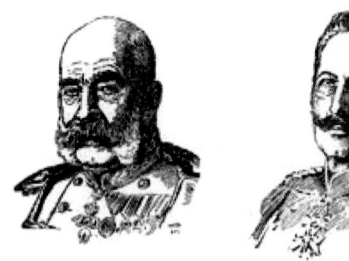

Newspapers in Germany and the United States announce the Declaration of War.
For a translation of parts of the article shown on the left hand side above, please turn to page 12.

was actively considering the deliberate violation of this neutrality. Germany only needed an excuse to put her plan into effect.

Prince Otto von Bismarck, first Chancellor of the newly united Germany had predicted that if Europe was ever to be thrown into war again it would be ignited by 'Some damned foolish thing in the Balkans'. How right he was. On 28th June 1914 the Archduke Franz Ferdinand, the Austrian heir apparent, was carrying out a state visit to Sarajevo, the capital of Serbia, when he was assassinated by Serbian nationalists. Austro-Hungary, a crumbling but still ambitious empire, used the occasion to march into Serbia as it had previously done in Bosnia and Herzogovina in 1909.

In 1909, the Russian army had been soundly beaten by the Japanese, leaving her in no state to go to the aid of her Slav neighbours. By 1914, however, she was determined to take aggressive action. On 28th July 1914, Russia declared war on Serbia and the following day besieged Belgrade. Austria reacted by mobilisation for war, whereupon Russia in her turn mobilised her vast army of six and half million men.

The Russian army of 1914 was poorly equipped and appallingly led. However, in spite of its serious shortcomings, its virtually inexhaustible supply of manpower made it a very real threat. Germany had treaty obligations to Austria and, on 31st July, Germany issued an ultimatum demanding Russian demobilisation within twenty four hours. No reply was received and, at 5 pm on 1st August Germany declared war on Russia.

France and Russia had signed a treaty in 1892, obliging each to move against Germany should either become involved in a ' defensive war'. Accordingly, when Germany declared war on Russia, France immediately mobilised. Germany was thus given her long awaited excuse to put the Schlieffen plan into effect and attack France.

Great Britain held back from the abyss. She was not a signatory of the Franco-Russian treaty, and, whether or not she had a moral duty to go to the aid of France, she certainly had no legal obligation. The Cabinet was split. Sir Edward Grey, the Foreign Secretary, believed fervently that Britain's interests required her to support France. However, the majority, supported by the Opposition, felt strongly that becoming entangled in other nation's wars should not be part of our foreign policy. Belgium however, was a different matter. Britain had been instrumental in setting up Belgium as a neutral sovereign state in 1839, and had a long standing treaty obligation to come to her aid should this neutrality be violated. The implementation of the von Schlieffen plan did just that. When at dawn on 4th August German troops crossed the Belgian frontier, Britain issued an ultimatum that unless they were withdrawn by midnight she would go to war. No reply was received.

At 4 pm on 5th August 1914, the Prime Minister announced to a packed House that Great Britain was at war with Germany.

Translation of the German Newspaper account for August 5, 1914
The full text of the announcement runs to nearly 1300 words. Translation by H.Yang, Spring 2011.

Germany declares war on England. Also at war with France.

The World War is in full swing. Germany and Austria stand alone against England, France, Russia, Serbia, Montenegro. Emperor Wilhelm's Momentous Speech from the Throne; All of Europe is now up in arms. Germany and Great Britain have declared war on one another. Germany formally decided that it considers itself to be at war with France.... The declaration of war was the result of Germany's refusal to acknowledge England's demand for respecting of Belgian neutrality. The British ambassador in Berlin has received his passport. Emperor Wilhelm holds an extremely important speech from the throne at the opening of the Reichstag. He describes the reasons why Germany decided to enter the war, and he expresses his confidence that Germany will be victorious.

The British Foreign Office issued the following statement: 'Since the German government has summarily rejected Britain's position that Belgium's neutrality should be respected, the British ambassador to Berlin had received his passport. The British government declared to the German government, that from 11 PM on August 4th, there exists a state of war between Britain and Germany.'

Emperor Wilhelm's Important Speech: Berlin, Aug. 4- at today's opening of the Reichstag:

"The world was a witness, as we have tirelessly attempted to protects the nations of Europe from a war between the large powers, to the chaos and unrest of the preceding years. The greatest threats had been created by the events on the Balkan Peninsula. Then came the murder of my friend, Archduke Franz Ferdinand, which opened a deep precipice. My ally, Emperor Franz Joseph, felt obligated to resort to weaponry to protect his realm against the dangerous agitation that was spread in a neighboring country.

While Austria-Hungary wanted to pursue its interests, Russia placed itself in their way. Our duty as an ally called us to Austria's side, and simultaneously a tremendous task was imposed on us. Together with the old culture of the two kingdoms, we had to protect our own position against the attacks of hostile forces. With a heavy heart I gave the order to mobilize my army against our neighbor, with whom we've fought side-by-side on many battlefields, and with deep regret I saw the destruction of friendship, to which Germany has kept so loyal. The imperial-Russian government, led by insatiable Nationalism, is taking aside of one of the states in the war, which has caused the calamity of this war by its criminal acts.

The fact that France has taken the side of our enemy came as no surprise to us. Too often our hopes for engaging in more friendly relations with the French Republic were met by the expression of old hopes and historically rooted hatred. The current situation is not born out of a temporary conflict of interest or diplomatic combinations, but is the result of growing envy at the years of strength and prosperity of the German Empire. We are not motivated by a yearning for conquest. We are propelled by the unwavering desire given to us by God to protect ourselves and to preserve our place for posterity.

My government, and in particular, my Chancellor, tried until the last moment to prevent it from progressing to the worst. We were forced into self-defense, and, with a clear conscience and clean hands we take hold of the sword.

I am making an appeal to the people and race of the German Empire. Together with our brotherly allies, we can defend what we have created in peaceful collaboration. Following the example of our fathers, strong and loyal, austere and chivalrous, humbly before our God and prepared for battle in the face of the enemy, let us trust in the Almighty, who gives our defense strength, and it will lead us to a fulfilling end."

Following the Emperor's speech, Dr. von Bethmann-Hollweg made the following short speech:

"We knew that France was ready for an invasion. France could wait, war or no war. However, an attack from the French to our flanks on the Lower Rhein would have been fatal, and that is why were forced to disregard the legitimate protests of the Luxembourg and Belgian governments. We will make amends once we have achieved our military goals."

2: The Conduct of the War

The principal protagonists in the Great War were also the greatest industrial nations of the World. This vast industrial potential that could be harnessed to the military machine was a new historical phenomenon. The sheer scale of manufacturing capacity meant that the size of armies which a nation could mobilize, equip and maintain in the field was only limited by the total manpower available, and the ability to produce munitions in unprecedented quantities rendered these armies capable of fighting battles of almost indefinite length.

In previous wars, battles had seldom lasted for more than a day. Problems of re-supply and the immediate availability of reinforcements rendered long battles impossible; history abounds with instances in which the victorious side was unable to exploit its success, often due in part to problems of supply.

In the Great War, battles were fought with the most appalling intensity over periods not of days, but of months. The Battle of the Somme lasted four and a half months and that of Third Ypres three and a half months. During these periods, millions of shells were expended - shells that could neither have been manufactured nor transported to the front a few years previously.

Industrial technology also provided armies with weapons of far greater destructive power. A field gun of the South African War period was fired over open sights at ranges seldom exceeding 1,000 yards. Because it had no recoil system it had to be manhandled back into position and relaid between each shot, which made its rate of fire extremely slow. Finally, the shells that it did deliver to its target were comparatively puny. Compare this to the devastating medium and heavy artillery of the Great War which could transform villages, woods and farmland into totally unrecognisable moon-scapes. It was not the rifle or machine gun that ruled the battlefield but the remorseless impact of high explosive shells, delivered in hitherto undreamt of concentrations by highly sophisticated artillery pieces.

However, communication systems had failed to keep abreast of the advancing technology of war, and were totally inadequate to control these vast new armies fighting long drawn out battles. Although radio existed, it never achieved any real significance in the field during the Great war.

Communications at all levels were primarily carried out by telephone. In a battle of any intensity the lines were soon cut by shellfire, and in spite of the valiant efforts of the linesmen, telephonic communication was for the most part inoperable. This meant that front line commanders relied on runners, that gallant band of largely unrecognised heroes who criss-crossed the killing zone of every battlefield, carrying vital messages. Even if runners were not killed or wounded, they frequently lost their way in the chaos of destruction; if they arrived at their destination, their progress was always painfully slow, especially at night. This inability to communicate meant that battles had to be pre-planned in great detail. There was no question of a commander briefing his officers on the opening phase of an operation and saying that, depending on its outcome, he would then issue further orders; by that time all communications were likely to have broken down and no more orders could be issued.

Battles throughout history have never gone according to plan; this did not greatly matter in the past when the scale was so much smaller and the general, mounted on a good horse, could gallop quickly to any critical point of the field where he was able to exercise personal control. This was not possible by 1915, when, once a battle had been joined, formation commanders were virtually out of touch with their units. The scale was too great for the whole affair to be watched from a vantage point, and in any case, the sheer deadliness of the 20th Century battlefield made it impossible for a general to follow closely behind his troops. This led to serious inflexibility in the conduct of battle, with no reliable method of changing a plan to meet changing circumstances. Under these conditions battles almost inevitably became hard slogging matches in which casualties were heavy.

The 1st Battalion Duke of Cornwall's Light Infantry entraining at the Curragh, Ireland, en route to France, 13th August 1914

3: The British Forces

The British Army of the Great War was made up of four distinct elements operating in one of three types of force. A chart and glossary of army organisation is set out on page 88 and those following it.

By 1918, the common experience of battle had tended to blur earlier distinctions and produce a homogenous force, but individual origins remained apparent to a greater or lesser degree.

1. The Regular Army

In 1914, Britain had a small regular army of a professional standard which has probably never been equalled. Unlike every other European army, it was composed entirely of volunteers. The soldiers were mostly young men who had enlisted for twelve years, of which six or nine were served with the Colours (ie with military units) and the balance on the Reserve (ie as civilians who were liable to recall in time of war). Officers came from the upper middle and upper classes. Their pay was minimal, many relying on private incomes, but their duties in peacetime were not arduous and their perks considerable. Leave allowances were generous by any standard, and often the only officers present in a barracks at a home station would be the adjutant and the orderly officer (both subalterns). Officers believed that there was nothing wrong in delegating routine matters to an extent that might be frowned upon today; thus subalterns learnt to accept responsibility far beyond their years and non-commissioned officers became experienced in commanding companies and platoons. This ability of junior officers and NCOs to instinctively take over when their superiors had been killed or wounded was to have a profound effect in battle.

Officers were expected to know a great deal about their soldiers and to look after them in a paternal way. The social gap between officers and men was, however, very great and soldiers would have been most unhappy if their officers had displayed undue familiarity. Discipline was strict, but everybody knew exactly where they stood and felt more comfortable for this. The military skills and attributes of a 1914 officer were not as demanding as those required today, but one failing, however, could never be accepted - lack of courage. Courage was considered the essential quality of every officer. In peacetime it was nurtured by the very real dangers of racing, hunting, pig sticking and big game hunting. In the Great War, these officers followed the tradition of the British Army by leading from the front and attempting never to show fear in public. Regular battalions also maintained their rigid codes of discipline even when in the front line trenches. Indeed, as Robert Graves points out in *'Goodbye to all that'*, discipline in action, however irksome, was absolutely vital if unnecessary casualties were not to be sustained.

One has only got to read Kipling to realise how the British private soldier was despised by the general public before 1914. Red coats were often refused service in respectable public houses, and enlistment was considered to be the last resource of a man desperate for work. In spite of or possibly because of this social ostracism, soldiers established extraordinary bonds of loyalty and comradeship within their units. If the Army was considered of little significance to the British soldier, the close bound family of his regiment most certainly was. It was this pride, unique amongst the armies of Europe, that inspired such dogged determination and courage in battle. A soldier would face almost certain death rather than let his regiment down.

A troop train carrying DCLI soldiers to Le Cateau in August 1914

The old regular army was virtually destroyed in the first battles of the war; Mons, Le Cateau, the Aisne, First Ypres and Loos all took a terrible toll. However, the men who had been dubbed by the Kaiser as that 'Contemptible little Army' changed the course of history. Not only did they buy vital time which allowed Britain to raise a citizen army, but, in the opening weeks they frustrated the German strategy - the von Schlieffen plan - to capture the Channel ports and attack Paris from the West.

When the regular army crossed to France in August 1914, it represented the best trained and most efficient army in the World. Throughout the war, the men of the regular battalions considered themselves an élite, taking a fierce pride in their professionalism and rocklike discipline. This pride existed in spite of the fact that very few of the original officers or men survived. The pre-1914 British regular army was a remarkable and unique institution with an ethos that was able to stand four years of total war.

2. The Territorial Force

The Territorial Force had been formed in 1908 from the Rifle Volunteers which had, in their turn, been raised in 1859 to counter the threat of French invasion. The primary role of Volunteers had always been the defence of their homeland; their compulsory deployment overseas was specifically prescribed by Act of Parliament. In 1908, Lord Haldane, the Secretary of State for War, foresaw the likelihood of Britain's involvement in a European war; he therefore made plans for Territorials to take over the Colonial garrisons in order to release regular troops for the European conflict. Thus it was that in August 1914 large numbers of volunteers from the Territorial Force set sail for India,

Africa and the Middle East. Their intended role was as garrison troops, but as war spread to Palestine, Salonika, Mesopotamia and the Dardanelles, more and more of these men found themselves in action against the Turks in the Middle East theatres. Many territorial units did eventually see action on the Western Front but they were the exception rather than the rule.

The Territorial Force was very different to the Regular Army. Apart from a regular adjutant and quartermaster, its officers were drawn from the professional classes - solicitors, bankers, land agents and accountants - with a sprinkling of the landed gentry. The men came from a wide cross section of society, their common bond being an enjoyment of comradeship and a liking for the outdoor life. As Territorials were essentially civilians who put on their uniforms once a week, discipline was exercised on a very different basis to that of the regular army and was certainly much more relaxed. It is difficult to judge the pre-war Territorials' efficiency at this distance in time. Although it would be most unfair to describe them as amateurs playing at soldiers, their military proficiency was undoubtedly far below that of the regular army. When they were mobilised, Territorial units required considerable additional training to render them fit for war.

3. Kitchener's Army

No detailed plans existed in August 1914 for the raising of a new volunteer army to augment Britain's regulars. However, as the scale of the forthcoming conflict quickly became apparent, Field Marshal Lord Kitchener was given the task of organising, recruiting and training a citizen force of a magnitude far greater than had ever been known in our Country's history. Everybody must be familiar with the poster which shows the heavily moustached Field Marshal pointing his finger at the reader, under the caption - 'Your Country Needs You'. The reaction to the appeal far outstripped the most optimistic forecasts. The recruiting campaign was launched on 6th August 1914 and by the end of the following year 2,466,719 young men had offered their services. The entire military training machine was, for a time, totally swamped by the huge numbers who came forward. Not only was there insufficient accommodation, clothing and weapons but there was a serious shortage of officers, NCOs and clerks. Exhausted adjutants and quartermasters worked round the clock documenting, acquiring stores of every description, organising emergency cook houses and scouring their counties for ex-officers and NCOs who could

 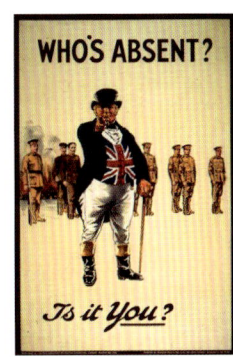

An example of the poster that became famous only after the war. The poster on the right was more typical of the many issued.

provide some sort of provisional command structure. Billets were requisitioned, tented camps rose from the fields and some sort of military discipline was imposed. Who were these recruits and why did they volunteer their services? It is probably true to say that the majority represented the cream of British manhood. Some may have enlisted because they were unemployed or disliked their jobs; some may have wished to get away from nagging wives or squalling children; some may have seen a chance to escape the debt collector - however, the vast majority appear to have left comfortable homes and secure jobs for reasons of patriotism. Young men of that period considered it their duty to answer the call to arms and fight a foreign aggressor.

A recruiting party trying to win converts to take the king's shilling in August 1915.

It was lucky that Kitchener's recruits were imbued with this enthusiasm, for their spirit was to be sorely tried over the next few months. Without uniforms, they trained and drilled in the civilian clothes that they happened to be wearing on enlistment. Administration was basic in the extreme and such things as the provision of food, blankets, and even pay, depended largely on the ingenuity and determination of Commanding Officers. Considering that many of the Commanding Officers were old men who had been hurriedly dug out of retirement, their energy, leadership and dedication were remarkable. Between the leaders and the led there quickly developed a spirit that was to overcome all obstacles.

The size of Kitchener's 'New Army' was enormous, far exceeding anything that Britain had previously raised. The Northumberland Fusiliers and the Royal Fusiliers each raised twenty seven battalions; the Middlesex and the Manchester Regiments, eighteen battalions; and the 60th Rifles raised sixteen battalions. The handling of a citizen army on this scale was an entirely new experience for senior regular officers; slowly it was welded into a force which, although still green and inexperienced, was deemed fit for battle. By mid 1915 the 'New Army' was beginning to cross over to France to reinforce the desperately hard pressed regulars.

One of the tragedies of the Great War was that these men who went to France with such high hopes, had of necessity to be committed to a major battle before they had gained sufficient experience. The battle of the Somme opened on 1st July 1916, the blackest day in British military history. From an attacking force of about 60,000, 56,000 men became casualties before nightfall. The battle dragged on for four and half months, each day adding to the terrible toll. The Somme devastated the 'New Army' in much the same way as the old regular army had been devastated by the great battles of 1914-1915.

4. The Conscript Army

It must be appreciated that up to 1st March 1916, every single officer and soldier in the British Army was a volunteer. However, by mid 1915, recruiting figures had fallen below the wastage rate and it was becoming apparent that conscription would have to be introduced if Britain was to keep a viable army in the field.

A recruiting party parading at Caerhays Castle, Cornwall, in 1915

The idea of conscription was new to this Country which, since the formation of a standing army in 1660, had always relied on volunteers. However, there was a growing feeling of unease that, while the cream of the Nation was being sacrificed in France and Flanders, many fit young men were content to remain at home often earning higher wages than those in uniform. In spite of this, there was certainly no unanimity over the issue. There were major divisions within the Government, Parliament and the general public; furthermore the TUC were militantly opposed to workers being conscripted to fight in what it considered to be a capitalist war.

Apart from this lack of agreement over the concept, there existed a very real practical problem - there was no National Register of the population, so that nobody knew the size of the potential manpower pool. Before the days of computers, the task of compiling such a register was monumental; a vast force of part-time volunteers had to be organised in order to deliver and collect the forms and then collate the information. In the event, the census showed that there were just over five million men of military age in the Country, of which only six hundred and ninety thousand were in jobs essential to the war effort. The theoretical manpower reserve was therefore enormous.

After considerable political debate, the Government succeeded in forcing through the Military Service Act on 27th January 1916. This allowed for the conscription of all unmarried males between the ages of eighteen and forty one, with the proviso that any person so conscripted could appeal to his local Exemption Tribunal. Initially these Exemption Tribunals were liberal in the extreme; during the first year of conscription 779,936 men were exempted while only 371,500 were compulsorily enlisted. By November 1918, in spite of a very considerable tightening up by the Exemption Tribunals, nearly half of the men who served in the British Army between August 1914 and November 1918 were volunteers. It may seem strange that at a time when Britain was engaged in the greatest war in her history, there should have been such a marked reluctance to implement a really effective policy of conscription.

The Fighting Arms

The operations of the army were divided into three main divisions:

1. The Artillery

The Royal Artillery had long prided itself on being highly professional. However, because guns, and more particularly shells, cost money, this arm was almost pathetically small when about to meet its forthcoming role from August 1914. The British Expeditionary Force embarked for France with 410 guns of which 322 were field guns, 16 were heavy guns, 72 were howitzers. Compare this to the French artillery strength of 4,000 guns. The field guns were of two types - 18 Pdrs with the infantry brigades and 13 Pdrs with the cavalry brigades. Both types were beautifully built weapons but neither fired a sufficiently heavy shell to have any significant effect against the entrenchments that would soon dominate the battlefield. In any case the only type of shell issued for field guns was shrapnel. This consisted of a light casing containing a large number of lead antimony balls together with a small bursting charge. It was a lethal weapon against troops in the open but useless against field defences. Furthermore, a very precise fusing system was required to ensure its detonation at the right height over the target; alas, British ammunition was often of poor quality and many shells either failed to explode or exploded at the wrong time in their flight. The vast number of unexploded shells that still litter the battlegrounds of France and Flanders testify to this shortcoming.

The 60 Pdr heavy guns and the 4.5in howitzers were both excellent weapons which were highly effective against field defences. However, with a combined total of only 88, they were insufficient in number to have any profound influence.

All guns were initially horse drawn, although steam traction engines and motor tractors were employed to move the heaviest pieces later during the war. Field guns, especially the lighter 13 Pdrs, could cross country at great speed, but then it only required one horse in the team to be killed or wounded to bring the whole detachment to a halt.

The industrial capability of this Country is well illustrated by the comparison of the 1914 artillery with that which was available for the Battle of the Somme in July 1916: in the preparatory bombardment leading up to the infantry assault, the British Army deployed 1,437 guns of which 427 were heavy, many far heavier than anything dreamt of two years earlier.

The use of any artillery piece depends on good communications between a Forward Observation Officer (who can see the target) and the gun line (which should be sited far back out of small arms range). In 1914, communication depended on a fragile telephone line, often cut by enemy fire in the early stages of an action. Guns were therefore employed right up within the infantry firing line, shooting over open sights while the gunners crouched behind the armoured shields with which all guns were then equipped. Weapons capable of throwing a shell eight thousand yards were thus being used at ranges of a few hundred yards;

A 13pdr gun crossing rough ground in 1918
(New York Tribune)

casualties were not unnaturally extremely high amongst the artillery men. The problems of communication were never properly solved until ground to air wireless equipment came into service during the last year of the war. This is why artillery programmes had to be pre-planned with such rigidity and why guns were seldom able to make quick switches to meet changing situations.

2. The Cavalry

The South African War of 1899-1902 had shown up the British cavalry as being signally lacking in professional ability. Not only had it lost an unnecessarily large number of horses through bad horse management, but it had been reluctant to admit that the sword was seldom an effective weapon against concealed riflemen. Reforms implemented after the South African war had done much to remedy these shortcomings and the British cavalry was probably the most efficient in Europe by 1914.

The role of cavalry was first and foremost one of reconnaissance; its secondary role was to harass the exposed flanks of an enemy; its third, but least significant task, was to ride down surprised or demoralised enemy troops. Although cavalry soldiers continued to carry swords till the middle of the Second World War, their primary weapon was the rifle. In 1907 all arms were issued with the .303in Short Magazine Lee-Enfield rifle, a highly effective weapon which was to remain in service, virtually unaltered, for another half century. The cavalry soldier's horse was his means of mobility; if there was fighting to be done he would generally fight dismounted using concealment and firepower.

In the early months of the war the cavalry played a full part in the mobile operations which symbolised that phase. As soon as the situation developed into the stalemate of trench warfare, their role as cavalrymen ceased to exist, although they were used as infantry in the front line. The aim of every major battle was to punch a clean hole through the enemy defences, through which the reserves could break out into open country. For this reason, a force of horsed cavalry was maintained behind the lines ready to exploit any such breakout. Indeed, in the last few months the war did finally revert to one of mobility. The cavalry again took to their horses but they never recovered their former glory. Technology had moved on. 'Whippet' tanks and reliable armoured cars could carry out the cavalry role more efficiently. For better or for worse, the mounted soldier had played his last part on the field of battle.

One must qualify the last few paragraphs by saying that, in the deserts of Palestine, horsed cavalry were used to considerable effect throughout the campaign. Sadly, it was because of its success in that theatre that the British Army was persuaded to retain horsed cavalry for the first three years of the Second World War, long after it had ceased to have any role in modern battle.

3. The Infantry

Mention of the Great War immediately conjures up a picture of the Tommy, begrimed with mud and filth, standing in waterlogged trenches, marching interminable miles loaded like a mule or attacking across the tortured moonscape of no man's land. This picture is not far from the truth. The infantry formed the largest part of Britain's army and suffered about four fifths of the total casualties. It often lived and fought under the most appalling conditions of mud, wet and cold, and yet maintained its morale in a manner that is scarcely comprehensible to our pampered generation. It would be difficult to argue that the British Infantry, by its determination, courage and robust humour was not a major, perhaps the major factor, in the defeat of Germany.

The regular infantry that went to France in August 1914 was a very small but highly trained force. Officers and men were all volunteers and formed part of a remarkably modern looking army. One should compare the British soldier in his drab khaki to the French soldier dressed in sky blue tunic and scarlet trousers, or the German soldier in field grey tunic with coloured facings and glinting brass spiked pickelhaube helmet.

Unlike the Germans, British infantry were taught to fight in widely extended formations. The South Africa War had been a bitter lesson and they had learnt to skirmish forward, using a tactic now known as fire and manoeuvre. German infantry still advanced en masse, shoulder to shoulder, presenting superb targets to the British rifles. The German staff had watched British infantry

A German cavalry trooper's helmet, whose wearer was killed by a DCLI soldier, probably the first shot by the infantry in the Great War.

tactics on exercises in 1912 and had concluded that men acting in isolated groups would never have the spirit needed to keep up the momentum of an advance. How wrong they were.

Officers went to war in August 1914 armed with a sword and .455in pistol. The sword was discarded in most cases before even the first shots had been fired. In many battalions officers carried rifles (principally so that they did not stand out as targets for snipers).

The infantry soldier's personal weapon was the rifle. Throughout the Great War, this was the .303in Short Magazine Lee-Enfield (or Rifle No1 Mk III* as it was officially known). Not only had the South Africa War proved the necessity for accurate rifle fire but the unique British experience against an elusive enemy on the North West Frontier of India had underlined the importance of marksmanship. Great importance was attached to a soldier's skill with his rifle and much time was spent on the range. The infantryman also carried a 17in sword bayonet, a ferocious weapon which probably did more to frighten the enemy than to kill him. However, bayonets were invariably fixed when in action and doubtless they were occasionally used to lethal effect.

From 1915, the British had the use of the Lewis light machine-gun. This was an American-designed weapon which had found no favour in the USA. The patents were eventually sold to Belgium and a small production line was set up in early 1914. The British, realising their need for a light machine-gun, removed the Belgian plant as they withdrew, shipping it back to England. The Enfield Small Arms Works

The .303 Lee-Enfield, No 1 mk 3, the finest service rifle ever built.

A Lewis Gun, the Enfield Small Arms Light Machine Gun, which became vital to British infantry tactics.

set up a major production line which produced hundreds of thousands of Lewis guns, many of which were to remain in service at sea throughout the Second World War. The Lewis gun gave the infantry platoon considerably increased fire power which enabled it to perfect the technique of fire and manoeuvre.

In 1914 the only infantry support weapon was the Vickers machine-gun which was initially issued on a basis of two per battalion. The Vickers was a superbly built weapon developed from the Maxim gun.

Training with a machine-gun in 1915

First issued in 1912, it remained in service, virtually unchanged, till the 1960s. Many are doubtless still being used in the remoter parts of the World. The Machinegun Corps memorial in Hyde Park bears the chilling inscription - *'Saul has slain his thousands, and David his ten thousands'*, which sums up the gun's terrible effectiveness in skilled hands. The Vickers was heavy, weighing 90lbs, and required a constant source of water to keep it cool; nevertheless it was the most efficient machinegun ever produced and could provide continuous fire for indefinite periods.

The infantryman of the Great War, whether regular, volunteer or conscript, developed a fierce pride in his regiment. The British Army was unique in fostering this very close feeling of comradeship in which every officer and soldier who wore a regimental cap badge was marked out as a member of the same elite family. This proud spirit was probably the principal factor that pulled men through the trials of battle and held groups of men together when chaos ruled around them.

This photograph from April or May 1917 shows four different fighting arms of the British Army:
(Front to rear): Infantry; a battery of 18pdr field guns; a tank; a squadron of cavalry in the background.

The Royal Navy

In 1914, the Royal Navy, although weaker than some thought prudent, was still a formidable force and by far the largest in the World. Its principal strength lay in the number of its capital ships.

In 1905, work with great secrecy led to the building of HMS Dreadnought, an entirely new class of battleship. Armed with ten 12in guns, with a speed of 21 knots, and protected by massive armour, she eclipsed any fighting ship previously built. Launched in 1906, she was quickly followed by nine further Dreadnought class battleships, and in 1910 by twelve Orion class battleships mounting 13.5in guns.

Meanwhile a new type of capital ship had been developed, the battle cruiser. These were armed with the same heavy guns as their battleship sisters, but carried less armour, allowing them greater speed. In 1914, Britain embarked on a programme of building super-Dreadnoughts armed with 15in guns, but these were not yet in service when war was declared.

In August 1914, the strength of the Royal Navy in ships was as follows:

- 21 Dreadnought class battleships
- 7 Battle cruisers
- 38 Obsolescent battleships
- 121 Cruisers
- 227 Destroyers
- 75 Submarines

The officers and seamen of the Royal Navy were generally considered to be the best trained of any in the World. These were 144,871 officers, seamen and marines on the active list, backed up by a further 51,836 on the Royal Naval Reserve.

A post card shows the Grand Fleet assembled at Spithead for review by King George V in July 1914. It gives some idea of why the Royal Navy was held in high regard and as an important element of national defence.

Most of the newer ships were oil fired which meant that they could be re-bunkered far faster than the older coal fired vessels. However, this did render Britain dependent on oil, principally from the Middle East.

This massive British naval force was able to bottle up the German navy in her home dockyards. Only once did it put to sea to fight a fleet action – off Jutland on 31st May 1916. For the four years of the war the Royal Navy ruled the North Sea imposing a rigid blockade on the German ports, denying that

A row of battleships in the 2nd battle squadron in 1914. Such great gunned ships played little part in the war and thereafter would become outclassed both by improvements underwater in submarines and in the air with airplanes and then aircraft carriers.

nation vital imports, especially of food. Blockading has always been a tedious and unspectacular operation, lacking the glamour and glory of sea battles. However, of all the factors that wore Germany down to final defeat, the North Sea blockade was probably the most important. Germany collapsed in 1918 because her population was starving.

HMS Acasta, a destroyer launched in 1912, was one of 20 in the Acasta class.
At the Battle of Jutland, 31st May, 1916, she operated with the Fourth Destroyer Flotilla. Holed fore and aft and in danger of sinking, she claimed to have torpedoed the leading enemy battlecruiser. In the painting above, the crew of HMS Acasta (the smaller vessel to the left) salute Admiral Jellicoe in HMS Iron Duke.

'Acasta was so damaged that she lay drifting close to the course of the British battleships. She had a list to starboard, two large holes just abaft the third funnel, one large hole forward on the port side, and sat very low in the water, her guns and torpedo tubes still trained abeam as they had been during the action. As the fleet flagship Iron Duke came by, firing her guns and leading her division, the men of the plucky little destroyer rushed out, forming a line from the forecastle head to right aft, and gave their Commander-in-Chief three hearty cheers. Acasta was afterwards taken in tow and brought safe to port.'

Painting reproduced by permission of Caerhays Estate

More than 5,000 allied ships were sunk by U-boats during the war. Such U-boats were submersibles with smoke stack and breathing tubes rather than submarines. The postcard illustation shows the famous German submarine SM U-9, which sank three British cruisers in less than an hour in September 1914. The picture on the right is number L27, an example of the more advanced British submarine.

Submarines developed during the course of the war into tactical weapons, with new forms of warfare required to defend against their secret attacks. It was only after reported submarine attacks on US shipping (and perhaps the sinking of the RMS Lusitania by submarine) that President Wilson of the US reluctantly entered the war on 6th April 1917. Although the submarine threat may have helped bring the USA into the war, their full potential as a force of war was not fully realised until the Second World War some twenty five years later.

Britain's Air Arm

In 1912 the Royal Navy and the Army established the Central Flying School on Salisbury Plain. Britain led the world in her belief that aeroplanes and airships could play an important role in any future war.

In the same year, 1912, a Short S38, the first aircraft ever to be launched at sea, took off from a temporary ramp built over the forward gun turrets of the armoured cruiser HMS Hibernia. Photographs show an extraordinarily flimsy machine with air filled floats which enabled it to land on the sea and be recovered. However, by 1914 many of Britain's capital ships carried float planes of various types which could be used for scouting. Several Naval air stations were also established around the coast. Nevertheless, the main effort of the Royal Navy was given to the operation of lighter than air machines, both dirigible and rigid. A functional dirigible had been tested in 1905 and the first rigid naval airship was built in 1911, although it never actually flew. Dirigibles proved ideal craft for submarine spotting and by the end of the war 158 had been built.

A postcard shows an early plane and balloon at Stonehenge

In July 1914, only a month before the outbreak of war with Germany, the Royal Naval Air Service and the Royal Flying Corps both obtained official recognition, thereby forming two separate air forces.

A Vickers FB5 Gunbus of 1915: An early and ineffective plane

The more effective Sopwith F1 plane at the end of the war, complete with guns firing through the propellor.

The Royal Flying Corps (the 'RFC') entered the Great War with only four squadrons of slow, unarmed aircraft. In spite of this, they performed miracles, shadowing the deployment and movements of the German army, and keeping GHQ informed of the situation on 'the other side of the hill'.

By the end of the war the design, construction and operation of aircraft had improved to such an extent that the RFC had been split into separate wings specialising in air to air battle, photo reconnaissance, bombing, and artillery spotting. This last role, which had previously been carried out from highly vulnerable moored hydrogen filled balloons, was, with the advent of wireless, of inestimable value. For the first time in history, artillery spotters were able to speak to the gun line and order instant corrections.

During these first years of the war, the naval wing, the Royal Naval Air Service, had also gone from strength to strength. On 2nd August 1917 the first ever deck launch and landing was carried out on the converted battle cruiser HMS Furious, (although the pilot was killed attempting to repeat his achievement the following day).

It was not until April 1st 1918, that the two flying services of the Royal Naval Air Service and the Royal Flying Corps were amalgamated to form the Royal Air Force. By 1918, this new Royal Air Force could boast enough planes for 150 squadrons, a very different organisation to that of the two small services and the simpler planes operating at the beginning of the war.

An attempt to mount a rifle on a french parasol monoplane at the beginning of the war demonstrates the ineffectiveness of the early planes.
Such planes had no ways of firing at each other and could do little damage. Pilots were reported as trying to throw grenades, use single shot rifles or fire pistols at each other, to little effect.

Source Gallica: Bibliothèque Nationale de France

4: Phases of the War

Although the Great War may appear to have consisted of one long hard slogging match between contestants who were dug into virtually impregnable field defences, the reality is that it can be separated into phases, each of a very different nature. These can be summarised as follows:-

Phase 1. The War of Mobility

In our parochial way, we have come to imagine that the clash of arms between Field-Marshal Sir John French's British Expeditionary Force and General von Kluck's 1st Army at Mons on 23rd August 1914 was the opening battle of the Great War. Nothing could be further from the truth. For the previous fortnight, fighting had taken place on a titanic scale involving seven German armies against five French and one Belgian army in Lorraine, the Ardennes and Charleroi. Known as 'the Battle of the Frontiers', this first phase of the war had been far from static. French military ethos could have been encapsulated by the word 'élan' and all teaching of that period was based on the principle, 'Attack is the only method of Defence'. All the early fighting consisted of wide, sweeping manoeuvres interspersed with violent and bloody battles.

Mons was the final engagement of 'the Battle of the Frontiers'. It took place on 23rd August on the extreme left flank of the allied front. It was fought too late because, by 23rd August, the French 5th Army had already fallen back, leaving the British Expeditionary Force dangerously exposed. Sir John French had no alternative but to retreat - fast.

There is absolutely no doubt that the tiny regular British Army fought with magnificent valour and skill on that day. It is right that the soldiers who took part should hold the Battle Honour 'Mons' in almost reverential pride, but in the context of 'the Battle of the Frontiers' it was insignificant. The battle of Mons lasted nine hours; two British divisions with a total of about 35,000 men were involved (only General Smith-Dorien's corps saw action) and these delayed General von Kluck's 1st Army of about 160,000 men for one day. This should be compared to the battles in Lorraine, the Ardennes and Charleroi which involved seventy French divisions with a total strength of about 1,250,00 men. The French suffered more than 140,000 casualties in these battles - twice the number of the entire British Expeditionary Force.

It was lucky that, due to a clash of personalities, von Kluck was forbidden to strike out west, outflank the British Expeditionary Force, and destroy it. In the event General French was allowed to escape south with his army largely intact.

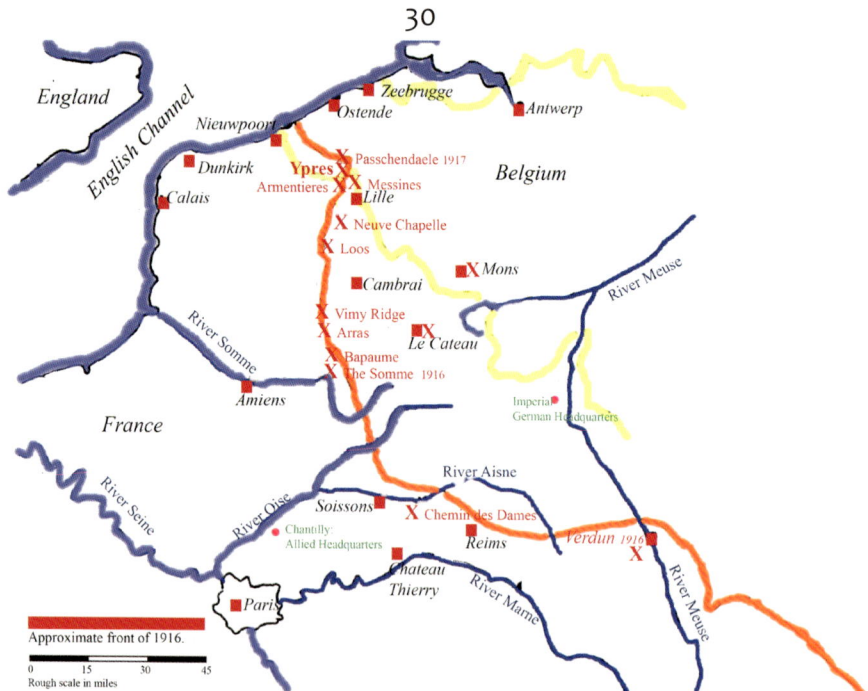

A sketch map shows the approximate positions of sites on the Western Front.

Sir John French had received explicit orders from Field-Marshal Lord Kitchener, the Secretary of State for War, that he must on no account risk the destruction of the British Expeditionary Force. This small army of two corps constituted almost the whole of Britain's trained fighting strength. At this stage there was no reserve. There is little doubt that Sir John French believed the campaign was lost, and, with the very real threat of being outflanked to both east and west, and directly confronted by four corps, he had good reason to look to Le Havre for the re-embarkation and evacuation of his army.

The British retreat from Mons must indeed take its place as an epic in the British annals of war. Retreat is a terrible destroyer of morale, but over the next fourteen days, the British Expeditionary Force withdrew 240 miles whilst maintaining contact with a numerically superior enemy. To simply march this distance in the hot August weather would have been no mean feat of endurance, but the British rearguard constantly halted to compel the advancing Germans to deploy into attack formations, before fading away before any attack could be mounted. During the retreat, General Smith-Dorien's corps were forced to fight a pitched battle at Le Cateau. Out of contact with Sir John French, and acting against the orders of his superior officer, Smith-Dorien took full personal responsibility to stand and fight. By his moral courage, he probably saved the British Expeditionary Force.

All this time, desperate fighting was continuing as the French slowly moved back towards Paris. But now the scenario was changing. Under the original plan, General von Kluck's 1st Army on the extreme right (north) wing should have carried out a wide encircling movement, capturing the Channel ports and investing Paris from the west. However, on 20th August, German GHQ, believing that the French armies were beaten, ordered the right to swing round to the south east and destroy the remnants of the French to the east of Paris. It was a fateful decision; the French, although desperately tired, were still holding together and fighting with great competence and tenacity. They were certainly not a routed army. Furthermore, the French were withdrawing into their own territory, so that they were adequately supplied with food, ammunition and supplies. The Germans, however, had outrun their lines of communication and, because bridges and railways had been destroyed in Belgium and France, were not only exhausted but starving. Towards the end of this phase, German soldiers were marching over thirty miles a day on the absolute minimum of food. One tends to think only of the hardships endured by the Allied armies as they withdrew south; these however pale in comparison to those suffered by the advancing Germans.

As the German flanking armies swung further and further over to the south east, so they exposed themselves to attack from the west. The consequent crisis occurred on 6th September. The French counter attacked on the Marne, forcing the Germans to withdraw north. Reluctantly, Sir John French was persuaded to support his allies and cease his remorseless withdrawal to the Channel. The British Expeditionary Force advanced to the north bank of the River Aisne where it dug itself in on 12th September 1914.

The hero of this phase of the war was the French Commander-in-Chief, Marshal Joffre. Throughout these terrible days, he almost alone had remained a firm rock, unshaken in his confidence in the fighting qualities of the French soldier. For thirty days, he provided vital leadership in a sea of seeming unending catastrophe, as he manoeuvred his armies with great tactical skill. He always listened attentively to his subordinate commanders and staff before making his carefully considered decisions. Quiet and solid, he could at moments of crisis exercise almost superhuman personal leadership. It was his passionate speech to Sir John French on the eve of the battle of the Marne that persuaded the British commander-in-chief to abandon the retreat and then attack in support of his allies.

History has not been kind to the British commander-in-chief, Field-Marshal Sir John French. He was thrown into this epic struggle with an army which, although highly trained, was minute in size compared to the immense French and German conscript armies. With instructions from the Secretary of State for War, Field-Marshal Lord Kitchener, that the army he commanded was the only army that Britain could put into the field, and that its survival was of absolutely overriding importance, it is perhaps small wonder that following the disastrous Battle of the Frontiers, Sir John French's primary concern was the safe evacuation of the British army from mainland Europe rather than the support of his allies. There was undoubtedly a grave conflict of aims. But it has to be said that Sir John French was not a commander-in-chief to inspire confidence. As a cavalry officer in the South African War he had shown considerable dash, but he was hopelessly out of his depth commanding the British Expeditionary Force. Quite unlike Joffre, whose cardinal virtue was to remain imperturbable in all weathers, Sir John French was impulsive, easily swayed by gossip, over responsive to pressures and possessed of a foul temper. As was said of him 'he displayed all the worst traits of an Irishman and a cavalry soldier'. His mind was closed to any form of intellectual pursuit and, by 1914, was less renowned for mental ability than for irritability. If this

Pte C. S. Perkins, 1st Battalion DCLI, in the trenches at Quique Rue, September 1914

was not bad enough, he disliked the French and spoke hardly a word of their language. However, the imponderable question will always remain - did the commander-in-chief, by his constant refusal to be drawn into the great French battles of August 1914, keep the British Expeditionary Force intact so that it could play its key role at Ypres.

Phase II. The Race to the Sea

Towards the end of September 1914 Sir John French suggested to General Joffre that the British Expeditionary Force should be withdrawn from the Aisne and transferred to its original position on the left flank of the Allied line. This would place the British in a stronger position to attend to the security of the Channel ports (so vital to their survival) and significantly reduce the length and complexity of their lines of communication. The idea was welcomed by Joffre, and plans were immediately made for the withdrawal of the three British corps from their position, sandwiched between French formations, on the Aisne.

The move of the British Expeditionary Force commenced on the night 2nd/3rd October and was carried out in complete secrecy (the Germans were totally unaware of the operation until the British re-appeared again in the north). It was a most complex manoeuvre which demonstrated the professionalism of the British regular army commanders, staffs and soldiers. The British had to withdraw unseen from a three corps frontage, cross the French lines of communication at right angles without disrupting their operations, link up with the northernmost French formation and then carry out a wheeling movement, against German opposition, in order to reform the British Expeditionary Force as a continuation of the French northern flank.

At the same time, a naval division, hastily assembled by Mr. Winston Churchill, First Lord of the Admiralty, was landed at Antwerp with the dual aim of supporting the hard pressed Belgian garrison, and effecting a link up with the main body of the British Expeditionary Force. This division, made up of one brigade of Royal Marines and two brigades of seamen who had volunteered for the venture, started to land on 3rd October, coinciding with the withdrawal of the British Expeditionary Force from the Aisne. Because of the naval division's almost complete lack of training, and total absence of heavy support weapons, the whole operation proved a fiasco. Antwerp fell to the Germans on 8th October. Part of the British force crossed the border into Holland where it was interned; the remainder became prisoners of war.

The defence of Antwerp delayed the advance of the Germans army by a few days, and gave time for the destruction of the port petrol handling facilities and the scuttling of some forty ships, rendering the docks unusable for many months. These, however, were expensively purchased gains. In every other way, it represented the disastrous loss of a division which, at that stage, Britain could ill afford.

On a lighter note, the Antwerp operation gave rise to one of the most ludicrous rumours of the war - that of Russians with snow on their boots. It was said that 80,000 Russian troops had landed in Scotland and been transported down the east-coast by rail to be re-embarked for Belgium. Dozens of self-styled witnesses swore they had seen these mythical soldiers travelling south in troop trains; one railway employee even stated that he had swept snow fallen from the Russians' boots from the platform at Edinburgh station.

As the British Expeditionary Force extended the Allied left flank, so the German army continued to confront its every move. General Smith-Dorien's 2nd Corps initially took the brunt of the fighting around Armentières and at the battle of La Bassée. Meanwhile, General Haig's 1st Corps and General Pulteney's 3rd Corps were advancing toward Ypres to form the extremity of the left flank. There they made contact with the remnants of the Belgian army who held the last few miles to the coast. Thus the 'race to the sea' was over. The line, which was to remain virtually static for the next three and a half years, was established. The period of fast, wide sweeping manoeuvre was over, and a new era of what amounted to siege warfare between two firmly entrenched opponents was about to start. Throughout this 'race to the sea' the Germans had enjoyed enormous numerical superiority, and, using this superiority with great skill, had managed to keep one step ahead of the British Expeditionary Force. It was for this reason that, when the line finally stabilised, the Germans occupied the best positions. In particular, the Germans held the ridges overlooking the Ypres Salient - a tactical advantage that was to ensure the most profound consequences in the savage battles that raged there in the forthcoming years.

In the initial stages of the war, the British Expeditionary Force cannot have been considered as anything but a minor appendage to the vast French armies. Now, the British held the key part of the front. This 'Contemptible Little Army' was about to cover itself with undying glory, to hold its ground against repeated attacks by overwhelming enemy forces - and to be virtually destroyed.

Phase III. The First Battle of Ypres: 13 October - 22 November 1914

The British Expeditionary Force had re-deployed on the extreme left of the Allied line by 13th October 1914. The race to the sea was over and one of the most heroic, possibly the most heroic, battle ever fought by the British regular army was about to begin.

The British initially deployed two corps, (that is, about 70,000 men) but this was increased to three when General Haig's 1st Corps (which had been covering the move) further extended the left flank a week later. The Germans initially confronted the British with four corps. However, a reserve of a quarter of a million reservists were in the process of moving up to this section of the front, many arriving at about the same time as Haig's Corps. Thus the German force in the Ypres area was about six times larger than the entire British Expeditionary Force and could call on a huge preponderance of artillery, particularly heavy guns.

The ancient city of Ypres was of no particular strategical significance in itself (though it certainly had emotional significance to the Belgians as the last of their cities not occupied by the enemy). Its importance lay in its position as the key to the Channel ports. The Germans knew full well that, if they could only break through the thin British lines, their way was wide open to drive on west to Calais, Boulogne and Le Havre.

The period known as the First Battle of Ypres was in fact a succession of the most savage battles fought up and down the British front from 13th October to 15th November 1914. It is important to remember that the British Expeditionary Force, although small in size, was extremely highly trained. The lessons of the South African War of 1899-1902 had been well assimilated and, unlike the soldiers of conscript Continental armies, who fought in massed formations, the British soldier was trained to fight well spread out, using well practised fire and movement. The British soldier's skill with his Lee-Enfield rifle was proverbial; not only could he achieve a fair degree of accuracy at 800 yards but, more importantly, he could fire fifteen aimed shots a minute at shorter ranges. Last, but not least, the British peacetime system of delegating command meant the serjeants and corporals were perfectly capable of commanding companies and platoons when their officers became casualties.

From contemporary accounts, the course of the First Battle of Ypres took on the aspect of a confused nightmare. In the fog of war, regimental officers and soldiers seldom knew what was happening beyond their immediate fields of vision. All were desperately tired. Stunned and concussed by the ceaseless shelling, men stuck to their positions with almost unbelievable valour. Inexorably the casualties mounted, as battalions were reduced to company strength and companies were annihilated. It is perhaps invidious to pick out individual actions in such a battle, but the following examples perhaps demonstrate the remarkable tenacity displayed by every unit.

Soldiers sleeping on the fire step of an undamaged and well constructed trench at Ypres 1914/5.

Between 21st and 24th October, the 1st Battalion Welsh Fusiliers hung onto their position until relieved, by which time the battalion had been reduced to a quarter of its original strength and had lost twenty one officers, (and about 750 men from their original strength of just under 1,000).

During the same period, the 4th Guards Brigade held a line eight miles long (a brigade frontage was normally no more than 1,000 yards) against an enemy four times as strong and with at least six times as much artillery.

Through the daylight hours of 24th October a party of the 1st Battalion Gloucestershire Regiment of ninety men held an isolated position until it was annihilated.

On 30th October, the action around a hamlet called Kruiseik left the 1st Battalion Coldstream Guards without a single officer, while the 1st Battalion the Welsh Regiment lost 16 officers and 600 men.

The following day, Lieutenant Blewitt and a handful of volunteers manhandled an 18 pdr gun up the Menin road, under heavy small arms fire, until they were in a position to engage and destroy a German gun which had caused a large number of casualties.

As a final example, one must quote the repulse of the Prussian Guard on 11th November. On the express orders of the Kaiser, the élite of the German army - the Prussian Guard - was ordered to attack on a narrow front and smash its way through to Ypres. The Prussian Guard, 17,000 strong, attacked at 9.30 am in pouring rain, after an artillery barrage of unprecedented weight. Since the centre of the attack was directed at the 1st Guards Brigade, Guardsmen faced Guardsmen as they had at Fontenoy in 1745.

Led by officers with drawn swords, the Prussians came on in serried ranks, advancing shoulder to shoulder as if on a ceremonial parade. The 1st Guards Brigade, already severely depleted, poured their fifteen rounds per man per minute into the advancing mass before being forced to withdraw. Next, the 4th Battalion Royal Fusiliers, reduced to 2 officers and 100 men, took up the fight, and, as the Germans still came forward, the 1st Battalion Scots Fusiliers, 1st Battalion King's Liverpool Regiment, 2nd Battalion Highland Light Infantry, 1st Connaught Rangers and a Field Company Royal Engineers came into action, each in its turn taking its bloody toll. The German advance was finally stemmed by the Gunners as it was on the verge of overrunning the guns of the 16th Field Battery. As the gunners continued firing at point blank range, the adjutant mustered every driver, cook, clerk, farrier and orderly to form a defensive line. The attack finally lost momentum, and, when the battle was over, the bodies of the Prussian Guard lay in piles seventy yards from the gun muzzles. Help for the Gunners was at hand in the form of the 2nd Battalion Oxfordshire and Buckinghamshire Light Infantry. History was to repeat itself again, for at Waterloo their predecessors - the 52nd Light Infantry - had fallen on the flank of the French Imperial Guard and destroyed it. Now, in the late afternoon, as daylight was failing, the Light Infantry attacked a demoralised and depleted Prussian Guard. In a short engagement, involving the most savage hand to hand fighting, the Light Infantrymen threw the leading elements of the Guard into rout. The Northamptons, Connaught Rangers, Highland Light Infantry and sappers of 25 Field Company Royal Engineers joined the pursuit, giving no quarter.

German documents indicate that, during these eight hours of fighting, the Prussian Guard lost 1,170 killed, 3,991 wounded and a further 1,719 missing (most of whom were almost certainly killed). The final German fling had failed; the British still doggedly held their line. After a last crescendo of carnage, both sides were left exhausted, capable only of digging themselves in to the complex defensive trench systems which were to dominate the Western Front for the next four years.

In these thirty three days, the British Expeditionary Force, under Sir John French, had held the most vital part of the entire Western Front at a critical time against a numerically superior force. In doing so, it had paid a terrible price in blood. Everybody has heard of Mons; few know about the First Battle of Ypres, but it was not at Mons but at Ypres that the British Expeditionary Force achieved it greatest glory.

Phase IV. The Stalemate November 1914 - March 1918

After November 1914, both sides dug themselves in to ever more complex defensive positions. The popular conception of the Great War became a reality. Multiple lines of trenches, connected by a web of communication trenches and protected by virtually impenetrable fields of barbed wire, stretched unbroken from the North Sea to Switzerland. The combatant armies had all trained for a war of mobility, but, by the end of 1914, the battlefield was utterly static. Infantry operations were, for the most part, confined to patrolling, and there was little movement during the hours of daylight. Artillery, some of very large calibre indeed, remorselessly pounded the defences, destroying trenches and dugouts. The war had become a gigantic linear siege, and, like all sieges, the cost in human life was high.

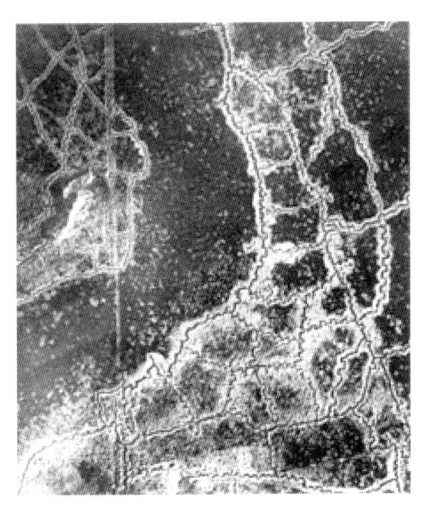

Aerial view of the Loos-Hulloch trench system in July 1917

Wars are never won by sitting passively in defence. The stalemate has to be broken by offensive action. The dilemma facing commanders on both sides was that attack against such formidable defences must inevitably be accompanied by very heavy casualties. These heavy casualties might be acceptable, providing success was achieved. However, the balance of war had tipped so heavily in favour of the defence that anything but the most limited success had become increasingly elusive. The war was in danger of becoming one of pure attrition. Each side was beginning to see its aim, not necessarily of gaining ground, but of wearing down the opponents' will to fight by the infliction of massive casualties.

A trench in winter 1916

This wearing down process again led to total stalemate. Once more commanders turned their attentions to major set-piece battles in an attempt to smash a breach in the enemy line which could be exploited by a mobile reserve. All through the late Summer of 1915, the newly raised battalions of Kitchener's army were arriving in France, swelling the British Expeditionary Force to a total of sixteen divisions.

Each nation in turn mounted massive offensives. First, the Germans attacked at Ypres. Using poison gas for the first time on 23rd April 1915, they drove in the British Salient till their leading trenches were within a mile and a half of the city. The battle raged non-stop for thirty-three days but Ypres never fell. Next, the British attacked at Loos, forty miles south of Ypres, on 25th September 1915. The British had no experience of large set-piece attacks and In spite of meticulous preparation, the result was a total disaster.

The French also mounted two offensives - one in the Artois area just south of Loos and the other in the Champagne area east of Paris. These operations recovered minimal ground at appalling loss - the Artois offensive cost the French 102,500 casualties between 9th May and 18th June 1915 and losses in the Champagne were 143,500 between 25th and 30th September 1915.

Soldiers of Ist Battalion DCLI at Neuve Eglise, January 1915, before cold weather clothing had been introduced.

The costly failure of the British at Loos was the final incident which led to Sir John French being relieved of the command of the British Expeditionary Force. He was replaced by Sir Douglas Haig. This change was welcomed by General Joffre who, with very good reason, had never trusted Sir John French. Joffre and Haig immediately started to lay plans for a combined allied offensive to take place in the autumn of 1916. This was never to be, for, on 21st February 1916, the German 5th Army attacked Verdun on a narrow front. Verdun, a fortress city on the Meuse, had a historical significance to the French which was probably greater than it actual strategic importance. The Germans gambled on Joffre committing all his reserves into this battle rather than see the city fall. They were right. Verdun was protected by thirteen massive forts which had been built in 1887; these were linked by a complex trench system. General von Folkenhaym (the Chief of the German General Staff) stated that the aim was not necessarily to break through but to draw in French resources and 'bleed France white'. Like Ypres, Verdun was never captured; the slaughter on both sides was however utterly appalling. French morale was destroyed, never to recover in the remaining years of the war. Germany, however, also suffered a sobering blow which sowed the seeds of disillusionment. In the three hundred days of fighting, her army captured a strip of totally devastated ground, just one sixth the area of the Isle of Wight, for which she paid the price of 330,000 casualties.

As a result of the cauldron boiling around Verdun, Sir Douglas Haig was brought under increased pressure to mount a major offensive with the aim of drawing the maximum number of German divisions away from the Verdun front. Thus was born the Battle of the Somme. The battlefield was centred around the town of Albert, some sixty miles north of Paris. This was not Haig's chosen sector but was willed on him by higher political authority, which decreed that the Somme offensive should be seen to be a combined British/French operation. The junction of the British 4th Army and the French 6th

Army at Bray-sur-Somme was therefore agreed as the proposed centre line of the offensive. In fact, because the French remained increasingly involved at Verdun, they were never able to play a major part in the forthcoming battle. The British Army, now heavily reinforced by the volunteers from Kitchener's New Army battalions, went into battle for the first time as a force on the Continental scale. On the Somme front alone, the British deployed some 230,000 men. The preparations for the battle involved training, rehearsal and staff planning on an unprecedented scale. Nothing was to be left to chance. On 24th June 1916, the British artillery launched a week's intensive bombardment - the heaviest ever in its history. Experts considered that an artillery preparation on this scale would cut the enemy wire, destroy his trenches and neutralise his guns. How wrong the experts were. At 7.30 am on 1st July, the British guns lifted and the infantry went forward. The wire had not been cut; the German guns had not been neutralised; more important, most of their infantry, although terribly shaken by the bombardment, were still alive. As the British guns lifted, the German survivors emerged from their deep concrete bunkers to fight. It is estimated that about 60,000 British infantry crossed the start line that morning; by dusk 57,540 of these men were casualties.

DCLI officers in France in 1917. Casualties among officers were high. Six weeks was the life expectancy of infantry subalterns.

The battle raged on, not for a day, or a week, or a month, but until 18th November 1916. Individual actions took on the magnitude of battles in their own right. Copses, reduced to matchwood and piles of rubble which had once been villages, were fought for with bloody intensity. Thiepval, Courcelette, Flers, High Wood, Delville Wood, Ginchy, Trones Wood and Guillemont are some of the names that became immortalised in British military history.

As the November weather rendered further operations almost impossible, the Battle of the Somme dragged to its conclusion. The British casualties were 420,000 (mostly young Kitchener's New Army men who had enlisted with such enthusiasm less than a year before); the Germans lost 437,500 and the French, 203,000. Statistics on this scale are difficult to comprehend. The Somme frontage was only about twelve miles long, but it witnessed the death or wounding of over a million men in four and a half months of fighting. The British Army paid a high price, but it learnt lessons that were to stand it in good stead in the final phase of war. It was only in the following year that the

Sandbag embrasures at Ypres in 1915,
where it was often impossible to dig trenches.

full impact on the German army became apparent. On 25th February 1917, in a masterly disengagement operation, it withdrew a distance of between 10 and 25 miles to a previously prepared defensive position known as the Siegfried-Stellung Line (or the Hindenburg Line as the British called it).

In June 1917, the British army, again under intense duress from the French to relieve pressure on their sectors (part of the French army had mutinied), agreed to another offensive, this time in the Ypres Salient.

Operations opened with the brilliant attack and capture of the Messines Ridge. Sir Douglas Haig is condemned for not following this success up with sufficient alacrity, but this judgement ignores the almost insuperable problems that existed in 1917 of moving reserves forward fast enough to catch the enemy still unbalanced. The Third Battle of Ypres started in earnest on 31st July 1917. British and Dominion troops pressed forward making slow but steady progress. Once again, as on the Somme, shattered woods and villages such as Langemarck, Glencorse Wood, Inverness Copse, Tower Hamlets, Polygon Wood, Sanctuary Wood and Broodseinde passed into British history. By the beginning of October, the Passchendaele Ridge lay within the Allied grasp. Passchendaele is a deeply emotive word which has become synonymous with the brutality of war. The battle opened on 12th October, in torrential rain, but was called off the following day because ground conditions, appalling at the best of times in the Salient, rendered movement impossible. On 26th October, a strong wind having somewhat dried out the ground, operations were recommenced. There then followed some of the most terrible fighting of the war. It was not only the resolute German defence which had to be endured, but the constant cold and wet. As one regimental history states, "life was not at its best when a moment's inattention could cause a man to slip into the filthy slime filled craters and drown".

The ruins of Passchendaele were finally captured on 10th November 1917.

Phase V. The German Offensives, 21 March - 17 July 1918

     By the winter of 1917-18, a profound war weariness had settled on the major protagonists. Germany, although still immensely strong militarily, was suffering the effects of three and a half years of British naval blockade so that her civilian population was on the brink of starvation.   The Austro-Hungarian Empire was breaking up due to internal national conflicts. Bulgaria was already negotiating a unilateral peace, and Turkey was experiencing mass desertions from her army. In the Allied camp, Russia was fast collapsing. Italy, in spite of being reinforced by British troops which could be ill spared from the Western Front, was finding herself hard pressed. France still held the largest part of the Western Front, but had been bled white by the continuous war of attrition. Britain was not only running out of manpower but supplies were coming under increased pressure from German submarines which threatened her lifeline across the Atlantic. The only gleam of light for the Allies came from the USA which had at last entered the war on 6th April 1917. American soldiers, inexperienced as they were, were starting to arrive in France.

     On 3rd March 1918, Russia surrendered under the terms of the Treaty of Brest-Litovsk. Germany immediately started the transfer of over a hundred divisions from the Eastern to the Western Front, thereby achieving an overall numerical superiority of 4 to 3 in the west. Both sides were only too aware that Germany must attack at the very earliest opportunity, if this numerical superiority was not to evaporate in the face of mounting US Army strength.

     Thus, three weeks later, at dawn on 21st March, Ludendorff's armies struck with devastating power against the British 5th Army in the Somme area. At 5.00 am, 6,000 German guns put down the most concentrated barrage in history. This was immediately followed by an assault of forty two divisions on a fifty mile front. Within days the British line was driven back forty miles, and ground won over months and years of fighting was lost in hours. It was, however, by no means a rout. Although the fog of war covered the battlefield, cohesion was somehow maintained in the apparent chaos. Filthy, exhausted and hungry soldiers kept up the fight. If separated from their own units, they joined up with anybody who happened to be there, and followed anybody who could display leadership. Men frequently fought their way back through encircling German forces, and artillery men often had to turn their guns through 180 degrees to fire on enemy attacking from the rear. Cooks, clerks and drivers joined the battle. Once more, the British soldier demonstrated his remarkable tenacity when faced by overwhelming odds.

     Throughout this period, headquarters struggled with the nightmare of controlling a major battle in which communications had broken down and the exact position of units was seldom known. Somehow commanders and their staffs managed to retain a grip on what must sometimes have appeared to be a rope of sand. Throughout the chaos, the basic logistical services continued to operate. Soldiers in the front line continued to receive the wherewithal to fight and casualties were efficiently evacuated.

On 11th April 1918, Sir Douglas Haig issued his famous Special Order of the Day:

"To all ranks of the British Army in France and Flanders:
"Three weeks ago today the enemy began his terrific attacks against us on a fifty mile front. His objects are to separate us from the French, to take the Channel Ports and destroy the British Army.
"In spite of throwing already 106 Divisions into the Battle and enduring the most reckless sacrifice of human life, he has as yet made little progress towards his goal.
"We owe this to the determined fighting and self-sacrifice of our troops. Words fail me to express the admiration which I feel for the splendid resistance offered by all ranks of our Army under the most trying circumstances.
"Many amongst us are now tired. To those I would say that Victory will belong to the side which holds out the longest. The French Army is moving rapidly and in great force to our support.
"There is no other course open to us but to fight it out. Every position must be held to the last man; there must be no retirement. With our backs to the wall and believing in the justice of our cause each one of us must fight on to the end. The safety of our homes and the freedom of mankind alike depend upon the conduct of each one of us at this critical moment."
D. Haig. F.M.
Commander-in-Chief British Armies in France.
General Headquarters, Thursday, April 11th 1918.

Meanwhile, further south in the Aisne, another massive German offensive was driving the French 6th Army towards Paris. On 26th March 1918, with the British/French gap widening and the Germans shelling Paris, a crisis meeting was held at the Hotel de Ville in the small town of Doullens. Those representing Great Britain were General Sir Henry Wilson (Chief of the Imperial General Staff), Lord Milner (Member of the War Cabinet), Field-Marshal Sir Douglas Haig (Commander-in-Chief) and four of his five Army Commanders. France was represented by M. Poincaré (President of France), General Petain (Commander-in-Chief), and General Foch (Chief of the General Staff). After a most dramatic meeting, during which members periodically withdrew for private discussion, the following joint statement was proposed:

"General Foch is appointed by the British and French Government to co-ordinate the action of the British and French Armies around Amiens. To this end, he will come to an understanding with the two Generals-in-Chief, who are requested to furnish him with all necessary information".

To the surprise of all, this did not go far enough for Sir Douglas Haig who announced that it presented Foch with too narrow a brief. He therefore put forward a counter-proposal that:

"General Foch shall be placed in control of the Allied Armies from the Alps to the North Sea".

This was agreed by both Nations. It was a momentous decision. In eighteen words, it healed the scars inflicted by the British failure to support the French in 1914; it restored French pride giving France control of a foreign army that had been operating independently on her soil; and most important, at that critical moment it ensured the vital unified command of the British 5th Army and the French 6th Army. Nobody could say that Sir Douglas Haig had not displayed magnanimity of the highest order, but he had also displayed great shrewdness, for, with the French in overall command, Foch had no choice but to commit himself to moving French divisions to support the hard pressed British 5th Army.

By 5th April, the German offensives against the British 5th Army and French 6th Army in the areas of the Somme and the Aisne had been brought to a standstill. Then on 9th April a third offensive was launched against the British 2nd Army in the area of Ypres. Once again, Foch moved French divisions to help meet this threat. An advance of some fifteen miles was achieved in places and the German line came within small arms range of the ramparts of Ypres itself, but the Germans had over stretched their resources and were unable to follow up their initial success. Germany's final fling had failed. Now was the time to strike against a demoralised enemy and finish the war.

Phase VI. The Advance to Victory

The final phase of the Great War was essentially achieved by the forces of the British and the British Dominions. In August 1914, the single British army was a mere appendage to the might of the five French armies deployed in the field. Now the British themselves had five armies; still a slightly smaller force than the French, but one that had become as professional as any in the world. It was the British and Dominion soldiers who took the brunt of the final battles and who led the Allies to victory. By the latter part of 1918, France, wearied and drained by four years of war, was no longer capable of a major offensive. The US Army, although rapidly increasing its strength in Europe was still lacking in experience.

The immediate requirement for the allied armies was a period of operational stability which would allow formations to be taken out of the line. Virtually every single unit had been heavily mauled, leaving it in urgent need of rest, reinforcement and re-equipment. Apart from this, there was a need to retrain the armies for what was already perceived to be the final phase of the war - the breakthrough battles followed by the pursuit. Very few officers or soldiers then serving had ever experienced anything but trench warfare; now the allies had to anticipate mobile operations in open country. The armies needed to be taught a totally different tactical concept and taught it with all possible speed before the Germans recovered.

By the end of May 1918, 750,000 US troops had landed in France. The British Army scented victory and its morale was high. Even General Petain, in one of his rare displays of optimism announced, "If we can hold on until the end of June our situation will be excellent. In July we can resume the offensive; after that victory will be ours".

It is a peculiarity of the British that we care to dwell on our disasters rather than our triumphs. The final battles of the Great War were triumphs of the highest order, yet few could name a single one of them.

Tentative attacks were made in July 1918, but it was not till 8th August that the full weight of the Allies fell on the German line in the Battle of Amiens. General Rawlinson's 4th Army composed of the British 4th Corps, the Australian Corps and the Canadian Corps, with elements of the French 6th Army, attacked at dawn along a twenty mile front between the rivers Somme and Avre. Rawlinson was a general who although perhaps not over gifted with imagination, had the capacity to analyse past failures and learn from mistakes. He believed that a cloak of secrecy was absolutely vital to the success of his offensive operations and that the enemy must be given no premonition of the time or place of an attack; to this end he devised the most elaborate deception schemes. Over 1,000 additional guns and 604 tanks were secretly moved into the battle area without the knowledge of the Germans. Meanwhile, noisy and visible preparations were made further north which successfully confused the enemy.

Many aspects of this attack were novel and presaged the tactics of 1939. The attack opened at dawn after a heavy but brief preliminary artillery bombardment. As the infantry went forward, they were closely supported by an entirely new generation of tracked armoured vehicles - 120 tanks converted to carry supplies and 22 tanks fitted out to transport two machine gun sections each. Immediately to the rear, 96 fast whippet tanks and a similar number of armoured cars waited ready to exploit any breakthrough. The operation was a complete success; by dusk that evening, a salient seven miles deep had been driven into the German line, and by 29th August 1918 the entire Anglo/French front along the Somme valley had advanced twenty miles. The Allied advance to the Rhine had begun.

Victory at the Battle of Amiens had been won with a very modest toll of casualties. The reasons were partly technical and partly the product of tactical analysis and sound training. Tanks were still mechanically unreliable, but battle drills had been evolved to ensure close armour/infantry co-operation. More importantly, radical advances in gunnery had improved the effectiveness of

The 10th DCLI (Infantry Pioneers), and German prisoners, repair a broken bridge and recover a sunken gun, limber and horses. A wagon train passes in the background. Cambrae, August 1918

artillery support. Previously, attacks had usually been prefaced by protracted bombardments, sometimes lasting several days. These gave the enemy the clearest indication of where the attack was due to take place; they cratered the ground creating a major obstacle for the attacking infantry; and they usually failed in their principle object of destroying the enemy. When the barrage lifted just before the assault, the enemy were too often able to emerge from their deep bunkers and fight. Bombardment was now superseded by a carefully controlled creeping barrage, behind which the infantry advanced. Shells were fused to explode on impact leaving negligible craters to hamper the infantry. Neutralisation rather than destruction had become the order of the day. All this was made possible by the development of efficient wireless communication between aircraft and gunners. Airborne observers could now watch the progress of the battle and direct the artillery so that fire was brought down exactly where it was most needed. A combination of wireless communications, advances in gunnery expertise and the availability of reliable shells and fuses had transformed the art of artillery support. The training directives laid down that infantry should try to keep within 50 yards of the artillery barrage; so confident however did the infantry become in the competence of their gunners that, in practice, they frequently advanced only 20 yards behind the exploding shells. By the use of these new techniques and skills, mobility had finally been restored to the battlefield.

On 22nd August, the town of Albert was occupied by the British; on 26th August the Canadians captured Vimy Ridge; on 28th August the Canadians breached the redoubtable Hindenburg Line; and then on 30th August the Australians were at Peronne, a further twenty miles to the east.

To the Germans, however, these allied victories paled into insignificance before a series of developing catastrophes which threatened their whole strategical concept - the Quadruple Alliance of the Central Powers appeared to be on the point of collapse, with Austria negotiating for peace while Turkey and Bulgaria were about to capitulate. Throughout September, barely a day went by without news of major Allied advances. The magnificent fighting machine of the German Army was beginning to crack. German troops continued to perform their duty with loyalty, courage and skill right up to the hour of the Armistice, but they were now well aware that their war had been lost, and that their wives and children were starving. For the first time, long columns of German prisoners of war could be seen moving westwards to captivity.

Reading accounts of 'the last hundred days', by which the final Allied offensives came to be known, one is impressed by the leading part played by Australian, Canadian, and New Zealand troops. The question must arise as to whether, at this point in the war, our Dominion troops were better than those recruited from the British Isles. It is a question that can never be easily answered. By 1918 the supply of British manpower was running out; she was scraping the barrel for men, and statistics show the often appallingly low physical standards which were being accepted for recruiting purposes. Throughout the war, Dominion soldiers had shown themselves as particularly robust and brave individuals, who, when well led, were capable of magnificent feats of arms. In the final months, they were frequently employed as the spearhead in attacks, and acquitted themselves with the greatest honour. It is, however, a myth that all, or even most of the fighting was carried out by Australians, Canadians, and New Zealanders. Without detracting from the proud record of these Dominion soldiers, one must point out that the largest proportion of our army were home-grown Britons, and the majority of their divisions fought with at least equal skill and tenacity.

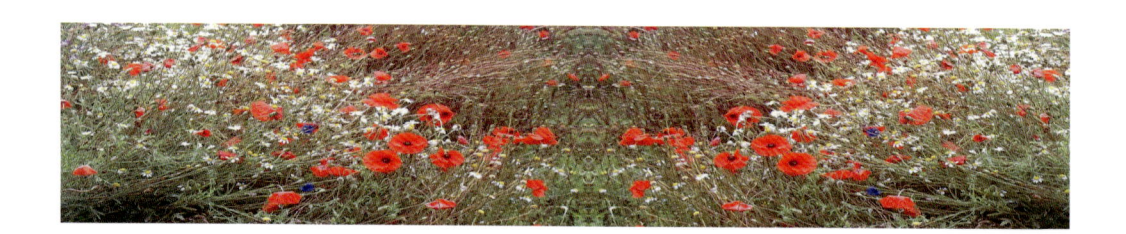

5: Generalship

Of all the aspects of the Great War, high command is by far the most contentious. Soldiers of every rank and historians of every persuasion have fuelled the argument for over eighty years and the young generation appear determined not to let the subject die.

In 1920 the senior commanders were held in the highest esteem by the Nation. It was not only the Establishment that supported them; they were also highly admired by the junior officers, NCOs and soldiers who had experienced the mud and blood of battle. When Field Marshal Lord Haig died, he was accorded a full military funeral in London and hundreds of thousands of ex-servicemen lined the streets to pay their respects to the man they considered to be a great leader.

However, during the late 1920s there was a radical swing of popular and academic opinion against generals. This was understandable; the country was going through a period of industrial depression and consequent mass unemployment; men and women became cynical and disillusioned as they saw 'a Land fit for Heroes' becoming one of poverty, hunger and loss of self respect. Generals were no longer the heroes who had led the Nation to a better life.

Let us look at the facts. All the senior commanders of the Great War were very experienced soldiers who had seen considerable active service in many theatres across the World. They had all taken part in the South African War of 1899-1902, a war in which Britain had been humiliated, but in which she had learnt many lessons. Between 1903 and 1907, the British Army had gone through a period of constructive soul searching. Every aspect of tactics, logistics and organisation had been carefully revised in the light of the lessons learnt. The sad thing was that the South African War and the war that Britain was shortly to fight on the Western Front could not have been more different.

The South African War theatre consisted of a vast area of veldt almost two thousand miles long by five hundred miles wide. There was no front line, only shadowy groups of a highly skilled enemy, which could move at great speed and were capable of inflicting heavy losses on an unwary force before melting away into the distant mists. The veldt was like a boundless ocean in which the adversaries manoeuvred like unseen ships. Mobility was all. Cavalry was in its element - not to carry out heroic charges, but to maintain contact with these elusive guerrilla bands and to fight dismounted actions using their rifles at long range. More horsemen were trained than ever before. Apart from the dozens of newly raised regiments of Irregular Horse, a significant proportion of the infantry was mounted, in order to give them greater mobility. Never before had the British army been involved in such a war of movement; it was a war that produced a well rehearsed tactical doctrine that was to prove singularly inappropriate by the end of 1914, leaving commanders trying to deal with a wholly unfamiliar scenario.

    The first month of the Great War was indeed one of mobility. The British Expeditionary Force carried out its remarkable fighting retreat from Mons to Tournan and subsequent advance to the Aisne. After that, all was changed. Both sides dug themselves into defensive trench systems which eventually ran continuously from the North Sea to Switzerland. Just twelve years after the South African War, we found ourselves embroiled in a static war. To the politicians and generals of Great Britain, France and Germany, this situation presented an almost insoluble problem. The aim was to defeat the enemy. To achieve this it was thought that an attack of such magnitude had to be mounted that it would break the stalemate and lead to the destruction of that enemy army in open battle. However, so powerful had the technology of defence become that not only were major attacks appallingly expensive in casualties but, until the last few months of the war, were never successful.

    Why were these attacks never successful? First, because a well sited, well entrenched defensive system, laid out in considerable depth with each layer of its defence protected by dense belts of barbed wire, offered an almost impregnable objective to attacking infantry (cavalry had long since ceased to be considered an arm of attack). Secondly, lack of an adequate communications system rendered senior commanders impotent to influence the conduct of a battle once it had started. If you look at operation orders produced during this period you will be immediately impressed by the incredible detail that they contain. Every eventuality was catered for; the programme of action, starting often many days before the first infantryman was to go 'over the top', was laid down minute by minute. This was fine, providing everything went according to plan; in battle this was seldom the case. Even before the first infantryman went 'over the top', units could be decimated by artillery fire or merely lose their way when moving up to their start line. Once the assault

Field-Marshal Sir Douglas Haig, KT, GCB, GCVO, KCIE, Commander-in-Chief, France, from Dec. 15th 1915.
Painted at General Headquarters, May 30th 1917 by Sir William Orpen, RA

had started, anything could happen. Usually it was setbacks caused by uncut wire or by unexpectedly fierce opposition; sometimes, however, formations or units could find themselves pushing all resistance aside and advancing far ahead of the programme. Each of these events was equally catastrophic; the commander seldom had the means of finding out what was happening in the forward edge of the battle, or, even if he could, of issuing new orders to adjust his overall plan.

We may criticise Haig for doggedly pressing on with major battles which we now know to have made little territorial gain at the expense of appalling casualties. Haig, Foch and Ludendorff all believed that the only way to achieve victory was to mount an overwhelming attack which would lead to a clear breakthrough. It is the tactics and not the concept that must be open to criticism. Haig believed that, provided he continued the onslaught long enough, the enemy would crack. He followed the Duke of Wellington's exhortation made at Waterloo – 'hard pounding Gentlemen. We will see who can pound the longest'. There is no doubt that Haig carried on with offensive operations long after the initiative had been lost and the battlefield had deteriorated into an impassable moonscape. It was not until after the Somme that vital lessons were learnt and that the tactical concept of clearly defined, limited objectives became standard practice. Marlborough, Wellington and Montgomery were all prepared to see a great deal of blood spilt in order to secure final victory. Generalship is not for the faint hearted.

Finally, and this is the basis of the historian John Terraine's argument, with which you may or may not agree, a junior officer or soldier can fight the battle and lose; providing, however, he has strained every sinew to the full and has shown courage beyond the call of duty, he can still hold his head high. Not so the general. He has been entrusted with the troops under his command for one purpose and for one purpose alone - to beat the enemy in the field. If he fails to do that, he has failed the Nation and failed his soldiers. Haig, against all odds, brought his army to final victory.

6: The Staff

No other part of the British Army of the Great War has been so vilified as the officers serving on the staffs of the large headquarters. They lived in considerable comfort behind the lines, out of artillery range. Unlike officers serving with their regiments, staff officers wore red bands round their caps, red gorgets on their collars and coloured arm bands. When these pristine gentlemen of the staff met Commanding Officers who had arrived straight from the front in their filthy, louse infested uniforms, the front line officers found the contrast too great to accept with equanimity.

The staff had never been popular in the British Army. It was firmly believed that an officer's foremost duty was to serve his regiment and look after the soldiers placed in his care. Officers who went off to the Staff College were little short of ambitious bounders! This ethos produced the extremely close knit family of a British regiment, but it set a divide between the regimental officer and the often very talented staff officer, which was far from healthy.

Headquarters at army, corps and divisional level were almost invariably accommodated in chateaux set several miles behind the front line, out of range of enemy artillery. These chateaux were not selected because they were luxurious buildings, but because they were the only buildings capable of housing the command, the staff and the throng of clerks, signallers, despatch riders, cooks, grooms and batmen which were necessary to run a headquarters efficiently. The sheer size of the armies of the Great War generated a volume of staff work never previously contemplated. Hundreds of thousands of men had to be billeted, fed, clothed, transported, paid, trained and kept healthy. When in battle, a vast and continuous supply of warlike stores had to arrive at the right place at the right time, fresh men had to be moved forward into the fray and casualties evacuated. The battles themselves were planned in the greatest detail and comprehensive orders disseminated to the fighting units. All this did not happen by magic; it was invariably the result of long hours of dedicated staff work.

Staff officers lived in some comfort, ate well and worked in comparatively well appointed offices. Only under these conditions could they have continued, month after month, producing the meticulous work that was so vital to the success of the fighting troops. Before the days of efficient radio it was vital that a commander should stand back from the front line and not become involved in the confusion of isolated battles. A headquarters represented the centre of a spider's web, lines of communication running back to higher command and forward to the fighting troops. Thousands of extemporary field telephone lines converged at the headquarters, whilst day

Lieut-Col D Borden Turner
A staff officer

Captain Darling demonstrated the image of a useless staff officer in the drama series *'Blackadder goes forth'*.

and night there would be a continual bustle of despatch riders and a coming and going of horses, motor cycles, cars and aircraft.

    Staff officers were never popular. Regimental officers considered their lives to be 'cushy', and resented the high proportion of decorations (now, quite rightly, only awarded for gallantry) that they received. Fighting soldiers, whose duties when 'resting' sometimes had to furnish the ceremonial guards on headquarters, felt strongly that they had enlisted to fight the Boche, not to stand rigidly, polished and preened, with rifle and fixed bayonet outside some smart chateau. Unlike the German Army, Britain had never had a professional Staff Corps. All British staff officers had their roots with the soldiers of their regiments, and, however rarefied the atmosphere at a big headquarters, few forgot the men who lived in the filth and danger of the trenches. Moreover, in an army not noted for its intellectual pretensions, British staff work was extremely efficient. Despite the near chaos of the March 1918 German Offensive, when the British Army was fighting for its existence, there was no collapse. Situation reports somehow got back to headquarters; orders were issued and the various logistic chains of supply, reinforcement and casualty evacuation continued to work. No other army was so well held together in the face of impending disaster during the Great War.

7: Destructive Weapons

Among all the weapons used in the Great War, the killing power of an artillery shell far outweighed all others. Both sides possessed large numbers of heavy and super-heavy guns which could obliterate trenches and destroy all but the deepest dugouts. British field artillery was initially only issued with shrapnel shell for use against troops in the open but by 1915 the British also had high explosive shell capable of damaging earthworks.

Whilst troops remained under cover in trenches, they were immune to rifle and machinegun fire. However, an attacking force had to move forward across open country where these weapons, but particularly the machine gun, could inflict terrible casualties. Troops in the open were also very vulnerable to the effects of shrapnel shell fired by artillery.

Mines, in the Great War context, consisted of tunnels and galleries driven deep under the enemy lines. Into these tunnels were packed large high explosive charges. The largest mine of the war, which contained 27 tons of high explosive, was detonated at La Boiselle on 1st July 1916. It blew a crater 450 ft in diameter and some 130 ft deep, and still holds the record as being the greatest non-nuclear explosion in history. Below all the major battlefields there existed a maze of tunnels. Both sides played a desperately dangerous game of mining and countermining in which small charges were frequently detonated in order to collapse enemy galleries. In the chalk area of the Somme, the intense heat and pressure of a mine detonation could react with the chalk (calcium carbonate) to produce carbon monoxide, an extremely toxic gas. The men on the surface appear to have had little knowledge about the drama being enacted below them unless a mine was exploded, usually creating the most appalling devastation. Mining formed an extremely important element of Great War tactics, and one which is now largely forgotten.

The enormous Lochnagar Crater, La Boisselle, Somme.

Poison gas was first used by the Germans in April 1915. It caught the French by surprise, causing a total collapse in their sector. Fortunately, the Germans were also unprepared for this success and failed to exploit their advantage. Within days of its first use, countermeasures were devised. The cotton pads then issued could be tied across the nose and mouth with tape. Crude as they were, they were reasonably effective. Pads were soon superseded by woollen gas helmets with glass eye pieces; they looked somewhat like Ku-Klux-Klan hoods, and were designed to be tucked inside the jacket collar. Both these devices were treated with a solution of sodium hyposulphate which acted as a filter.

Soldiers wearing the final model for respirators.

When the potency of the original chemical wore off they could be soaked in urine, which was almost as effective.

The use of poison gas was highly emotive, and it is largely due to this that the ban on its use has generally been maintained since 1918. In fact, it killed remarkably few men since it was easily detected, and so long as gas discipline was good, counter measures could be taken before any permanent ill effects were suffered. The first gas used was chlorine. It was released from cylinders in the front line and required a steady, gentle wind to blow it across to the enemy. Chlorine was a pungent greenish gas which was particularly dangerous in small concentrations but dispersed rapidly. In December 1915, phosgene (carbonyl chloride) replaced chlorine. This was also released from cylinders, but, unlike chlorine, was an odourless invisible gas which was many times more toxic than chlorine. It did, however, cause coughing and choking which gave a man time to don his respirator before serious harm could be done. It dispersed rapidly. The final agent was mustard gas (dichlorodiethyl sulphide). This was in fact a liquid which was deployed by artillery shell. The bursting of a mustard gas shell dispersed this liquid over a wide area in the form of a fine mist. Contact with the skin produced rawness, extreme irritation and suppurating blisters. Contact with the lungs produced excruciating pain and permanent disability or death. Mustard gas was highly persistent and traces remained floating on the water in shell holes for many months. From contemporary accounts, it appears that poison gas was accepted as just one more beastliness of war, but was certainly not feared in anything like the same degree as was artillery, machine gun or rifle fire.

The principal role of aircraft during the Great War was reconnaissance and artillery spotting. They were capable of dropping small bombs and shooting up troops with their machine guns. However, their guns were provided primarily for action between aircraft; it would have been a foolhardy pilot who took his fragile aircraft down sufficiently low to strafe infantry who could return his fire many fold. By 1918, reasonably reliable wireless equipment had been developed for aircraft, which formed the basis for a major advance in battlefield communications.

Barbed wire was, of course, a passive rather than an active weapon. It did, however, have a profound effect on battle and was largely responsible for the virtual impregnability of a Great War defensive position. Wire could be laid with unskilled labour and was almost impossible to breach with any degree of reliability. It made a mockery of the orderly infantry advance across no man's land and rendered any use of cavalry impossible. Wire was laid by both sides in enormous quantities. Apart from belts 200 yards or so deep across the front of the forward line, there were often similar belts between each succeeding reserve line. Yet more belts were laid running from front to rear to give units flank protection, and 'stops' consisting of bundles of barbed wire were suspended over the trenches at strategic points, so that, even if the enemy succeeded in occupying a portion of the line, he could be contained by letting the bundle of barbed wire drop into the trench. Barbed wire could be cut either by prolonged bombardment with shrapnel shell or by the use of bangalore torpedoes (lengths of steel pipe full of high explosive which were slid under the wire); neither was very effective. The tank was probably the only reliable method of crushing barbed wire so that the infantry behind could advance.

Two photographs give some idea of the near invulnerability of barbed wire entanglements.

Tanks were introduced ahead of the technology that was later to make them so formidable. They were slow, unreliable and too easily bogged down in the morass of shell holes and mud. They could be destroyed by field artillery, and even small arms fire, although not penetrative, knocked splinters off the inside of the armour. They did, however, carry considerable firepower (greater than that carried by British tanks in the years 1939-1943) and could undoubtedly use their guns most effectively when supporting infantry in the attack. As mentioned above, they provided the only reliable means of crushing barbed wire. Because of their novelty, and their sinister image as massive, lumbering, unstoppable machines, they were probably more feared than their performance warranted. The tank

The Mark 5 tank with 6pdr side guns

A tank in trouble, 1916. Note trench

was a British invention. The Germans quickly produced their own versions which were quite remarkably unsuited to the role. (A far cry from the extraordinary lead in tank design that they had achieved by the Second World War). By 1918 the British had developed fast, light Whippet tanks which largely usurped the role of cavalry in the final breakthrough.

A captured German anti-tank rifle

Grenades provided an important weapon in trench warfare. They could be lobbed into dugouts or over the top of traverses. Crude grenades, consisting of an iron ball containing gunpowder from which stuck a short length of fuse, had originated in the 18th Century. Design had hardly improved by 1914, when improvised grenades still consisted of a jam tin filled with explosive. By the following year, the mills grenade was produced. This had a cast iron shell segmented like a chocolate bar, which ensured that it broke up into a large number of fragments; it also had a simple and reliable detonation system which was a far cry from the projecting length of fuse. Means were later developed to fire grenades from rifles giving considerably greater range. The Mills grenade was an excellent weapon which continued in service for the next sixty years.

Firing a rifle grenade: June 1915

The 1915 N5 Mills Hand Grenade

The Germans used a different device consisting of a cylindrical can on the end of a wooden handle. Their tactical system often included waves of 'storm troopers' armed only with large numbers of stick grenades.

Bayonets, knives, daggers and spiked 'knuckle dusters' all played their part in trench fighting. One somewhat eccentric Commanding Officer of the Welch Regiment paid for the making of medieval Celtic swords which he then issued to his battalion for trench raids. Medical records appear to show that casualties actually inflicted by cold steel were minimal. However, the steel bayonet in particular was, and indeed still is, deeply symbolic of aggressive infantry action. A soldier with a fixed bayonet becomes imbued with a fighting spirit which gives this weapon an importance far beyond its killing power.

8: Living Conditions in the Front Line

For most of the four years of war the British held a sector of the front line which ran southwards from a point just north of Ypres in Belgium down to the north bank of the River Somme in France. To the north of the British sector lay the Belgians and to the south the French.

The front line ran through a wide variety of terrain which included rich farmland, industrial and coal mining areas, and derelict villages. The northern third of the British sector was dug into clay while the southern part was chalk. All troops in the front line were protected by trenches which over the years were developed into a highly complex defensive system usually sited in very considerable depth. The line itself consisted of forward trenches backed up by at least two parallel reserve lines set two or three hundred yards apart. These were interconnected with a network of communication trenches leading to the rear. Some of these communication trenches were extended back half a mile or so to allow movement to and from the front line in comparative safety. Saps, in the form of narrow trenches or tunnels, were also dug forward from the front line to listening posts often only a few yards from the enemy. Dugouts were hollowed out of the trench walls every twenty yards or so to give protection against artillery and to allow men to rest with some degree of safety. Latrines were sited in short spurs off the communication trenches. The 1915 manual of field defences recommends that a trench should be 9ft wide at the top, 3ft wide at the bottom and 6ft 6ins deep. Then, since a man could neither observe nor use his weapon in a trench of this depth, a 'fire step' was cut in the forward face, on which a man could stand. All trenches were dug in a zigzag pattern so that a shell falling in a trench would inflict only the minimum casualties. These right angle bends were

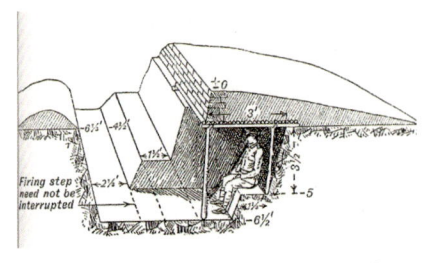

A 1912 manual shows the theory of a well made trench.

A picture of the reality from the Ypres salient in 1915

Another sort of reality: digging a communication trench at Delville Wood. The red line marks the line of the trench.

Left: Putting a mirror above the parapet;   Right: A rifle with periscope attachment.

known as 'traverses'. Trenches were drained by channels running into sumps and the trench floors were covered with wooden duckboards. The earth walls were revetted with sheep hurdles, corrugated iron, planks or any material that came to hand, while dugouts were shored up with substantial timbers. The construction of these earthworks with pick and shovel represented a huge and continuous task. Wide belts of barbed wire were laid along the front and between each reserve line, with small gaps left in the forward belt of wire to allow patrols and raiding parties to move to and fro. Further wire entanglements could be dropped into trenches to hinder the enemy exploiting a local success. The distance between the front line varied from between a mere twenty yards to half a mile.

    This was the situation - at least in theory. In practice, the front line varied so much that it would be impossible to describe it in general terms. In certain sectors - notably between the south of Arras and the northern edge of the Somme battlefield - there was virtually no serious fighting. The trenches, which were dug out of the firm chalk, never underwent heavy shelling and conformed fairly exactly to the specifications laid down in the manual. Life in this sector was therefore probably comparatively comfortable and not particularly dangerous.

    At the opposite end of the scale were the conditions in the Ypres Salient. This was not only clay country but consisted of a low lying area which, before the war, had been artificially drained. Four major battles of considerable duration were fought over the Salient, reducing it to a featureless stinking swamp in which rotted the bodies of thousands of men and horses. In many parts, the maintenance of any semblance of recognizable trench layout

DCLI troops by a dugout at Ypres in 1914-1915

became impossible. The front line degenerated into a string of flooded shell holes in which men existed as best they could. The provision of hot food and the evacuation of casualties was at the best difficult and sometimes impossible. This was the battlefield which was loathed and feared by soldiers, and which came closest to destroying the morale of both the British and German armies. It was a battlefield in which men literally sank without trace into the slime and mud.

Every sort of condition existed between these two extremes, but in most places heavy artillery fire destroyed the appearance of the neat diagrams in the training manuals.

The duration of a battalion's tour in the front line varied considerably depending on the operational situation, the availability of troops, casualties and the physical conditions that had to be endured. Once again, it is difficult to generalise on the length of a front line tour, but, from reading war diaries, it appears that a front line tour could vary between a couple of days and a month. The cold and wet were probably as potent a factor as the enemy, particularly where trenches flooded. Rubber thigh boots and goatskin jackets were being issued by the winter of 1915, which must have somewhat alleviated the misery.

Cooking up behind the lines at Ypres in 1915

The DCLI in reserve trenches at Ypres, 1915

In most sectors of the line hot food came up at least once a day. The menu of bully beef, biscuit, margarine, plum jam, tea and cocoa may have been monotonous but it was plentiful; the British soldier (unlike his German counterpart) was well fed. Rum was issued each evening. Two species of uninvited guests shared the trenches - rats and lice. Rats spread disease and were therefore killed by any means available. This included rat hunts which could provide light entertainment in quiet periods. Lice infested all clothing inflicting acute discomfort far out of proportion to their size. Fumigation plants were established in rear areas which provided temporary relief, but the problem was never solved and the itching of louse bites remained one of the enduring memories of Great War soldiers.

Men spent a comparatively small proportion of their time actually in the front line. Within a brigade of four battalions, the forward battalion would probably be deployed so that two of its companies were in the front line, with a company in the second line at immediate readiness, and a further company in the third line. The rear company would provide men for fatigues, carrying parties and patrols. Half a mile or so behind the front line would be a reserve battalion at immediate readiness to move forward. Behind that would be the second reserve battalion, probably living in cellars or buildings. This battalion produced a large labour force each night for carrying up defence stores and repairing shell damaged field works. Several miles to the rear, the fourth battalion would be resting in a town or village. The men lived in proper billets and enjoyed the freedom to visit bars and cafés, meet girls, relax, play games and catch up on lost sleep. Battalions moved through this cycle continuously until such time as their brigade was pulled out of the line for retraining.

Left: A trench mortar which, since it always brought retaliatory fire, was therefore an unpopular presence in the line; Right: Reassembling equipment; DCLI at Ypres 1914/5

A soldier's life was always hard, often uncomfortable and sometimes extremely dangerous, but it certainly did not consist of continuous action in front line trenches. During quiet periods in the line, the principal tasks were maintenance and improvement of the trenches and barbed wire, and patrolling. The first of these is self explanatory; the second needs comment. Patrolling was carried out for two reasons: first, to gain information; secondly, to foster an offensive spirit by dominating no-man's-land and generally harassing the enemy whenever possible. Patrols could vary in scale from major raids complete with complex artillery support, to a few men crawling out to the enemy front line. In the British Army almost all patrols, however small, were led by officers. Patrolling was, and still is, considered one of the principal duties of the junior officer. It was a very severe test of his courage; his performance, when only a few yards from the enemy positions, was watched and judged by the soldiers with him. Officers frequently crawled out across no-man's-land with only one or two other soldiers, and indeed there are many stories of their going out alone to lie immediately under the enemy parapet, or even creep about in the darkness of enemy trenches. Some men undoubtedly delighted in the excitement and danger of patrols; most probably accepted them as just one more unpleasant duty imposed on them by their seniors and were never more glad than when they regained the safety of their own trench.

Warning sentries of friendly activity to their front was not easy. Patrols often fell behind their planned timings or got lost and came back in through a neighbouring battalion; sentries changed every hour or so and it was only too easy for instructions not to be passed to reliefs. For whatever reason, returning patrols were not infrequently fired on by their comrades, often with tragic results.

A defining picture of the war in France:
Infantry advance over shell-pitted ground.
The Battle of Guillemont, Somme; September 3rd-6th, 1916.

9: Campaigns outside Europe

Although the vast majority of the Great War fighting took place on the Western Front, there were certain campaigns which were geographically far divorced from France and Flanders. These so called 'Peripheral Campaigns' fall into three categories and geographical areas:

    a.   The need to thwart the Turkish threat to the Suez Canal and the Anglo-Persian oil fields resulted in campaigns in Palestine and Shat-el-Arab, Mesopotamia.
    b.   After it had been perceived that the Western Front battle had become a stalemate, attempts were made to attack the Central Powers from the south with campaigns such as those at Salonika and Gallipolli.
    c.   A scarcely remembered war was waged in Africa between the colonial armies of Britain and Germany for four years.

The strategic importance of the first category was probably crucial, particularly in maintaining an Allied hold on the Suez Canal.

The campaigns in the second category were of dubious overall value. An attack on 'the soft underbelly of Europe' has seemed an attractive proposition in both World Wars, but in neither did it fulfil the expectations of its advocates. In the Great War, Haig believed that victory could only be achieved by winning the hard slogging match on the Western Front, and strongly opposed the dissipation of his forces to the peripheral theatres. With hindsight, one must agree with his conviction, particularly in view of the unmitigated disaster of the attempt to force the Dardanelles at Gallipoli. The Salonika and Dardanelles operations were part of the same overall campaign, launched against Bulgaria and Turkey on both the west and east sides of the Aegean Sea.

Operations in Salonika went ahead without undue risk. The British force landed at Salonika, a good deep water port held by an allied power - Greece. The subsequent advance north proceeded slowly and carefully, principally because the rocky terrain was particularly inhospitable and there were no roads. A large proportion of the force, together with Greek labourers and Bulgar prisoners of war was employed largely on building a road up the axis of advance. There were no great set piece battles; mosquitoes and the illness arising from that malaria brought by mosquitos claimed more casualties than the Bulgaria and Turkish enemy. Progress was made, and by 1918, British, French, Greek and Serbian forces had advanced into Bosnia, Serbia, Rumania and Bulgaria, reaching Sarajavo in the west, Belgrade in the centre and Varna on the Black Sea in the east. The Serbs were once more engaged against the

Southern Front of the German Army, and Turkey and Bulgaria had collapsed.

The third category of campaigns, fought almost exclusively by African Colonial troops in Togoland, Cameroon German East Africa and German South West Africa, were, perhaps, largely irrelevant to the outcome of the war. However, they tied down some 20,000 African Colonial troops who could have been used elsewhere and taught Britain two somewhat humiliating lessons: first, that the African soldiers from the German colonies fought a forlorn war against overwhelming odds with utter loyalty to their German officers; secondly, that the senior German officers, outnumbered and almost totally cut off from their motherland, conducted operations with the very greatest skill. The German colonial campaigns in Africa are worthy of greater study than they receive today.

The gallant and pathetic story of the Allied attempt to force the sea passage of the Dardanelles by capturing Gallipoli is the best known peripheral campaign of the Great War. Should it have succeeded, it would have opened the way to the Black Sea, outflanked Turkey and Bulgaria, and linked the forces of Britain and Russia. It not only failed, but failed disastrously. Too little was known of amphibious assault operations; once landed, the troops on the ground failed to exploit local success, due to the difficulty of communications.

The Palestine Campaign, 1915-1918

In February 1915, a Turkish Army under their German commander, General Baron von Kressenstein, attacked Egypt with the object of capturing the Suez Canal. The operation failed for logistical reasons. The subsequent withdrawal of the enemy main body had been a pitiful affair, with over a thousand dying of thirst in the desert.

On 23rd March, the Turkish rearguard which had held a defensive position opposite the town of Suez was routed. No follow up was attempted at this stage, the Commander-in-Chief, General Sir John Maxwell, very prudently refraining from committing troops to that merciless desert which was already destroying his enemy so effectively.

However, when winter came, preparations were started for advance into Palestine. Water pipes and light railways were laid out into the desert while, at the same time, small but significant raids were made, disrupting the enemy water supplies. Two of these are especially worth mentioning. On 20th February 1916, a long range air attack with a return journey of 200 miles, (perhaps the first in history), was made on the reservoir at Hassana Well, where a year's work by German engineers was destroyed in minutes. Shortly afterwards, a regiment of Australian Light Horse carried out a remarkable attack on the well at Jifjaffa. Marching 160 miles across waterless desert in three and a half days, they surprised the garrison, who were killed or taken prisoner, and blew up all plant and material.

In April 1916, the Turkish Army again advanced towards Suez. Fighting on this occasion was far fiercer, but the result was the same, and by May operations had once more ground to a halt. At the end of July, the Turks made their third and final major attack. After heavy fighting the Allies were able to advance along the whole front on 5th August, and on the 8th August the Turkish Army was heavily defeated at the Battle of Romani. General Sir Archibald Murray, who had taken over as Commander-in-Chief, was at last able to begin his advance to the east.

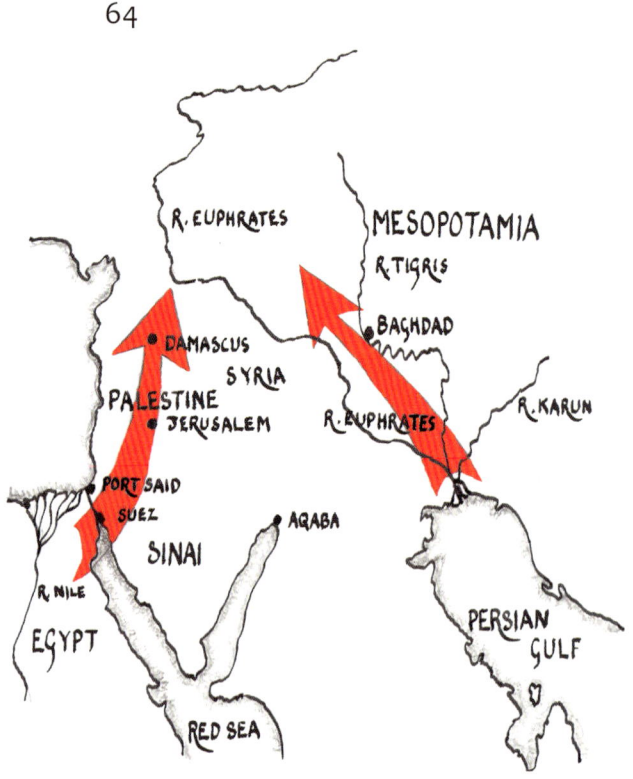

The Palestinian and Mesopotamian Campaigns

By this time, a considerable Allied force had been assembled in Egypt, consisting of British, Australian, New Zealand and Indian cavalry and infantry, together with a huge logistic train of camels. Stocks of railway material, water pipes and pumps were now at hand, ready to be pushed out into the desert behind the leading troops. The Allies advanced into the Sinai desert and by early January 1917 had entered Palestine. The ancient, and tactically vital, city of Gaza was reached by March. Gaza was, however, to prove a far harder nut to crack than any previous operation in this campaign. After two disastrous attacks, the Allies were left to lick their wounds, whilst General Murray was replaced by General Sir Edmund Allenby. Allenby moved his GHQ from Cairo to within a few miles of the front, improved the communications system with his army and imposed the strictest discipline of secrecy. By a series of ruses, he was able to outwit the Turks, who were completely misled as to his plan of attack. Gaza fell on 1st November 1917. Continuing the advance through the heavy winter rains, he entered Jerusalem on 9th December.

While Allenby regrouped and prepared for the final advance towards Damascus, the situation in France necessitated the transfer of almost the entire British element of his Army to the Western Front. There followed a frustrating period of ten months during which Indian troops were moved into the theatre and trained for the task ahead. On 15th September 1918, the advance was recommenced. Damascus fell on 1st October, and the Turkish army was trapped, 100,000 prisoners falling into allied hands. On 31st October, Turkey surrendered. In just over a month she had suffered a defeat that is arguably without parallel in modern history. Out of an army of nearly 3,000,000 men only 500,000 remained. Allenby's work was done. At a cost of less than 6,000 casualties, he had conquered the northern half of Palestine, the whole of Syria and had destroyed three Turkish armies. Few generals have ever achieved such a total victory. This was also to be the last campaign in history in which cavalry played a significant, indeed major, part. It was also the first campaign in which aircraft were regularly used in the close support role.

Although the robust endurance of the troops taking part must never be underestimated, victory depended to a great extent on the enormous work achieved by the Royal Engineers, in constructing the logistic infrastructure necessary to maintain an army operating in an utterly barren land. The railway which followed the advancing troops, and the network of water pipes, reservoirs and pumps must rank as some of the great improvised engineering works of the century.

The Campaign in Mesopotamia, 1914-1917

By 1913, the island of Abadan at the head of the Persian Gulf had become the source of much of the World's oil supply. The oilfields, which were owned by the Anglo-Persian Oil Company, were of vital importance to fueling the Royal Navy which, at this time, was changing from coal to oil firing in its ships. When war broke out in August 1914, it was therefore essential that the Abadan oilfields were secured against capture by Turkey. Accordingly, in November 1914, an Anglo/Indian force under Lieutenant General Sir Arthur Barrett was despatched to occupy Abadan and its hinterland to a depth of about 100 miles. His orders were to secure the oilfields whilst at the same time rallying the local Arab sheikhs to the Allied cause.

This initial limited aim was achieved with commendable speed and efficiency. However, the Commander-in-Chief India (who had overall control of the Mesopotamian theatre) then decided to extend the whole scope of what had originally been intended as a comparatively minor operation. He proposed no less a plan than a full scale advance up the River Tigris in order to capture Baghdad. The loss of this city by the Turks would undoubtedly represent a very severe body blow to the Central Powers. The original expeditionary force was therefore enlarged to the strength of a corps under the command of General Sir John Nixon. The 6th Indian Division under Major-General Charles Townshend was selected to lead the main thrust.

Blind optimism appears to have triumphed over military expediency. Certainly, with hindsight, it is easy to condemn Townshend for failing to face up to the inadequacies of his logistical support. In fact, his advance of some

300 miles up the Tigris, accompanied by a motley collection of river gunboats, tugs and lighters, was conducted with great efficiency. By 21st November 1915, he had reached Ctesiphon, a mere 25 miles from Baghdad. Here his luck changed when a German officer - General von der Goltz - took command of the opposing Turkish forces. In both the Gallipoli and Mespotamian campaigns it was a well proven fact that Turkish troops performed most effectively when under the professional leadership of German officers. Townshend was forced to fall back on the small town of Kut-el-Amara - an immensely strong, natural defensive position sited in a tight loop of the Tigris. There, on 9th December 1915, he was surrounded. Valiant efforts were made by General Nixon to effect a relief while, within the garrison, shortage of food, ammunition and medical supplies, together with the continual attrition of cholera, dysentery and malaria, were taking their toll. By February 1916 all supplies of vegetables, rice, sugar and tinned milk had been exhausted, and the following month the last of the horses and mules were slaughtered for meat. On 29th April 1916, the 9,000 Indian and British troops in Kut-el-Amara surrendered - the greatest single surrender of a British army since the capitulation to the Americans at Yorktown in 1781.

During that summer, control of the Mesopotamian campaign was transferred from the Commander-in-Chief India to London. Port facilities at the mouth of the Tigris were improved, lines of communication were strengthened, a fleet of suitable river craft was assembled and the medical organisation was overhauled and enlarged. Lieutenant-General Maude was placed in command, with the task of re-establishing a British presence at Kut-el-Amara as a preliminary to the capture of Baghdad.

Detailed plans were made to meet every foreseeable contingency and on 13th December 1916 General Maude struck north up the Tigris. In a masterly campaign in which he took the greatest care never to outrun his carefully prepared lines of communication, British and Indian troops occupied Baghdad on 11th March 1917. By the Summer General Maude had extended his conquests across the whole area bordered by the Euphrates and Tigris. Then, tragically, at the height of his achievement, he contracted cholera and died on 10th November 1917.

Operations in Mesopotamia had swung from wild optimism to deep despondency; from ignominious disaster to sweeping victory. In the long term, the campaign achieved its aims, which were initially to safeguard the Royal Navy's oil supplies in Abadan, and subsequently to capture Baghdad. The fall of Baghdad led directly to the surrender of Turkey on 30th October 1918. This itself was one of the factors that caused Germany to request an armistice on 11th November that year. In both defeat and victory, the resolution of the British and Indian soldiers never faltered. They operated in an environment which could scarcely have been more lethal or unpleasant. Disease-carrying mosquitoes abounded in the low lying Tigris and Euphrates valleys, while cholera and dysentery were endemic. In the early stages of the campaign, the medical facilities were wholly inadequate, the conditions under which the sick could be nursed were appalling, and disease accounted for the loss of far more men than had the enemy.

The Salonika Campaign, 1915

Salonika is probably the least remembered theatre of the Great War. The origins of the campaign lay in the two Balkan wars of 1912 and 1913 which, like all Balkan conflicts down the ages, were extremely complex. The initial cause lay in a demand by Serbia (a land locked nation) for the use of a port on the Adriatic coast currently within the domain of Turkey. Her aspirations were backed by two Christian nations - Montenegro and Greece - who saw this as a final opportunity to drive the Mohammeden Turks from their last hold in Europe. Bulgaria did not join this 'Balkan League', content to stand back and pick up Turkish territory to her south, should the situation develop favourably.

On 8th October 1912, Montenegro declared war on Turkey, whereupon Turkey declared war on the three other Christian nations - Serbia, Bulgaria and Greece. Turkey was quickly driven back till she held only a narrow strip of land in Europe, to the north of the Dardanelles and the Sea of Marmara. The fighting was temporarily suspended by an armistice signed on 12th December 1912. However, the following year, Greece, Serbia, Montenegro and Rumania turned against Bulgaria, whereupon Turkey, seizing the opportunity offered by the squabbling Christian nations, counter-attacked, taking back much of her lost European territory. The British Army was only marginally involved at this stage, merely providing medical units in Serbia.

At the outbreak of the Great War in 1914, Serbia came under attack from

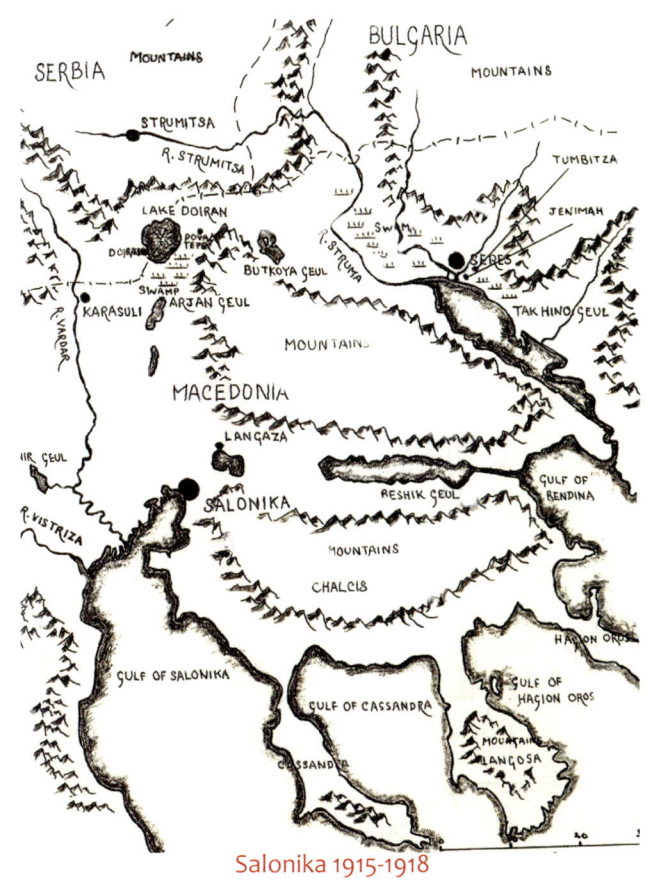

Salonika 1915-1918

the Central Powers of Austria, Hungary, Germany and Bulgaria. In 1915, Great Britain despatched a force to Salonika (by this time part of Greece) in a vain bid to save Serbia. It was too late. Russia had failed to break through from the north, and the Serbian army, ill-equipped and outnumbered, was forced to carry out a remarkable two hundred mile retreat through the mountains from Pristina to the port of Durazzo on the Adriatic, from where it was evacuated by Allied warships. Astonishingly the Serbs brought with them 24,000 prisoners of war (mainly Bulgarians). After extensive re-training and re-equipping, the Serbian army was then brought back into the fight on the Salonika front.

Meanwhile the British advance from Salonika made little progress. A large proportion of the force, together with Bulgarian prisoners of war, was employed on road building and other logistical duties necessary to maintain a modern army in the field. In the low lying, mosquito infested swamp land surrounding Lake Doiran, where most of the actual fighting took place, malaria incapacitated complete units and was responsible for more deaths than the enemy. It was not until the Autumn of 1918 that the French and Serb armies, under General Franchet d' Espèrey, broke through the Dobropolje Ridge and, making the longest and swiftest advance of the whole war, swept up the Danube, through the plains of Hungary, and prepared to march on Berlin by way of Budapest. By then, however, Germany had accepted an armistice.

The Gallipoli Campaign, 1915

By November 1914 it was already apparent that the situation on the Western Front was degenerating into a stalemate. Mr. Winston Churchill, the First Lord of the Admiralty, therefore made strong representations to the War Council to open a second front in the Middle East. Turkey had just declared war on the Allied powers and was geographically well placed to threaten the Russian Southern Front, the Persian oilfields and the Suez Canal. Churchill, a man whose imaginative concepts sometimes outran more practical considerations, argued that an attack on the Dardanelles - the very heart of Turkey - would neutralise these threats at a single blow. Furthermore, the capture of this narrow sea route would allow Britain to send much needed war supplies to Russia and provide support to the wavering eastern Balkan states which bordered the Black Sea.

The Dardanelles is a narrow strip of water which connects the Mediterranean to the Black Sea. To its north lies European Turkey and to its south, Asiatic Turkey. The channel, which is 30 miles long, varies in width from about three miles to only 800 yards. Churchill initially proposed that a combined operation, employing a number of heavy gun warships supporting a land force of 500,000 British, French, Italian and Greek troops should be mounted. However, the French army was fully involved in the defence of its homeland and the small British Expeditionary Force in Europe had taken such devastating casualties in the first months of the war that it was in no position to release a single soldier. In January 1915 the original plan was therefore radically altered and it was decided that the capture of the Dardanelles should be carried out as a purely naval operation.

At this time the Royal Navy had a superfluity of obsolescent battleships which, although too slow to work with the Grand Fleet, carried very heavy guns. A combined naval fleet was therefore assembled in the Mediterranean consisting of the new battleship, Queen Elizabeth, twenty old battleships, (fifteen British, four French and one Russian), together with an armada of destroyers and minesweepers. A Royal Marines battalion, trained in demolition, was embarked, which could be landed by small boat immediately after each bombardment to complete the destruction.

The fallacy of this plan lay in the fact that, in any age, it has never been possible to secure ground by means of bombardment alone. Ultimately, it must be occupied by infantry. Not only was the Dardanelles defended by massive fortress artillery, but there were innumerable smaller mobile guns, which could be concealed in tunnels and deep entrenchments when not in use. Furthermore, the Turkish artillery and engineer arms were largely officered by extremely capable Germans, who used the existing resources to the very best advantage, repaired damage with great skill and speed, whilst inspiring their Turkish soldiers with optimism. Last but not least, the Turkish navy had sewed the narrows thick with mines which the minesweepers, operating under constant close range fire, were never able to clear effectively.

The impracticality of the whole concept was made all too clear on 18th March 1915 when, within a few hours, three battleships were sunk and three more so badly damaged that they could take no further part in operations.

The fleet withdrew to lick its wounds. The failure of this first phase did much to raise the morale of the Turkish army which was seen to have taken on the might of the Royal Navy, and won. At the same time, any enthusiasm that the eastern Balkan states might have entertained for joining the struggle against Germany suffered a lasting blow.

Even before this fateful day, the War Council had become convinced that a purely naval operation could never achieve the aim. A re-appraisal was therefore made, and plans were laid for troops to be assembled at Mudros on the Greek island of Lemnos. The force was to be commanded by General Sir Ian Hamilton and was to consist of about 120,000 British, Australian, New Zealand and Indian troops together with a Royal Naval Division. General Joffre could not afford to release men from his hard pressed armies on the Western Front, but agreed to contribute 36,000 soldiers of the Foreign Legion and the African Colonial Army. Italy and Greece declined to become involved. Secrecy was impossible, and the build up of troops and shipping in Mudros Bay was watched closely by Turkish naval reconnaissance units.

The Gallipoli peninsula forms the northern shore of the Dardanelles. It consists of a rocky promontory some 30 miles long and 11 miles wide at its broadest point. In the Summer months water is scarce or non-existent, while in Winter the numerous dry stream beds become raging torrents. The whole area is contorted by steep ridges and deep ravines covered in thick thorny scrub - ideal defensive country. Furthermore, the topography of the Dardanelles left no alternative but for the landings to take place on the western extremity - a fact of which the enemy defenders were fully aware.

On 23rd April 1915, St. George's day, the invasion fleet sailed in an atmosphere of euphoric crusading ardour. The marine bands on the warships played, while cheer after cheer echoed across the waters as the crowded troopships nosed out into the open sea and headed for Gallipoli.

At 5.00 am on 25th April, the Australians stormed ashore at Gaba Tepe on the east coast, against very strong opposition. Moving inland against a withering fire, they scaled the cliffs and rapidly advanced to within a few hundred yards of the west coast. Had they established themselves across the width of the peninsula, the outcome of the campaign might have been different. Their numbers, however, were insufficient to meet the onslaught of the Turkish counter attack, and, without artillery or even machine guns, the Australians were forced to withdraw back to the perimeter of the original beach head where they were quickly joined by New Zealand and Indian reinforcements. Their situation was still desperate, but at dawn on the following day the Queen Elizabeth and seven old British battleships moved in close to the shores of Baba Tepe, where they were able to bring down very heavy fire on the Turks. Simultaneously, British troops were landing at four points on the southern extremity of the peninsula, while the French contingent occupied positions on the Asiatic shore of the Dardanelles at Kum Kale. Both these landings were fiercely contested and casualties were heavy. In what was later to be described as 'the most remarkable landing in military history', battalions of the Lancashire Fusiliers, the Munster Fusiliers and the Dublin Fusiliers went ashore from the converted collier, S.S. Clyde, at Sedd el Bahr. In capturing the near impregnable heights above the beach, the fighting qualities of this brigade became a symbol of all that was heroic at Gallipoli.

The British, ANZAC and Indian divisions had suffered appalling casualties in securing their narrow beachheads. Allied manpower and equipment could not easily be replaced, whereas the Turkish army was receiving massive reinforcements. Further advance became impossible. The stalemate that this campaign was specifically designed to break set in across the Gallipoli front as both sides dug in and waited.

With the onset of summer came the scourge of flies and vermin spreading disease; corpses infected the meagre supplies of water bringing cholera, enteric fever, typhoid and dysentery. Modest reinforcements were received but these failed to replace the wastage of killed, wounded and sick. To add to General Sir Ian Hamilton's worries, three battleships, Goliath, Triumph and Majestic were sunk on 25th, 26th and 27th May respectively. This loss resulted in the Royal Navy no longer being able to guarantee the security of merchant ships bringing in supplies of ammunition, food, medical supplies and water. The Allies launched a final fling using two fresh divisions at Sulva Bay, a few miles north of the ANZAC position. For once, surprise was achieved and the British secured a beach head without undue casualties, whilst the ANZAC and Indian troops in the Gaba Tepe salient made the most valiant efforts to establish contact. Due to a breakdown of communications, bad leadership and a lack of any sense of urgency amongst the British troops on the Sulva Bay front, this operation quickly ground to an ignominious halt. The corps commander, General Stoppard, was hastily removed.

In October, General Sir Ian Hamilton was also relieved of his command, being replaced by General Sir Charles Monro who quickly became convinced that there was no further object to be gained by continuing the campaign and that the entire allied force should be evacuated. Field Marshal Lord Kitchener visited the Dardanelles in early November and fully endorsed Monro's opinion.

The final decision to evacuate Gallipoli was made in the middle of December 1915. By this time 25,000 men had been killed, a further 12,000 were missing and 100,000 had died or been rendered ineffective by disease. The task of disengaging the allied force from its close contact with the enemy, and evacuating it under the Turkish guns, could not have been more daunting. In the event, this evacuation was successfully carried out with efficiency, perhaps the only part of this sorry campaign to rate unqualified praise.

During November 1915, all sick and wounded were evacuated, together with men and equipment not essential for the final phase of the campaign.

On 4th December the final evacuation of the beach heads commenced. By this time, the Turks were fully aware of the Allied intentions. The slightest breach of security would therefore have had catastrophic consequences. So every sort of ruse was employed to trick the enemy into believing, not only that the Allied positions were fully manned until after the final departure, but that the Allies had no intention of withdrawing until the Spring. The final phase started on the night of 18th December when three fifths of the force was evacuated. All through the following day the Allies waited tensely.

Silently the battleships lay off shore with every gun trained on the Turkish positions. In the front line trenches, the depleted garrison maintained occasional desultory fire whiled final preparations were made to activate the various devices which would continue to dupe the Turks into believing the empty positions to be fully manned that evening. As soon as it was dark, on the night of 19th December, the transports again moved into the beaches. By 3.30 am, all fighting troops had been withdrawn leaving only General Monro, his staff and a party of RAMC doctors and stretcher bearers on the Gallipoli shore. By 5.00 am, the last Allied troops were embarked. A number of brave midshipmen remained with their steam pinnace crews until dawn to pick up stragglers, but so efficiently had the whole operation been performed that not one man was left behind. Indeed, during those two nights, the entire force was evacuated without the loss of one single man, horse, mule or gun. Never before or since in history has an army been embarked under the noses of a superior enemy force with such total success.

This must be attributed to brave and intelligent leadership, brilliant planning, faultless co-operation between the Royal Navy and Army, a high standard of discipline which ensured complete secrecy and, last but by no means least, luck. The month of December is infamous for severe gales in the Aegean Sea, yet during the vital nights of 18th and 19th December 1915, the sea remained an oily calm.

African Colonial Operations, 1914-1918

Few people today know anything of the four campaigns which were fought in Africa throughout the years of the Great War. In 1914, Germany held the substantial colonies of Togoland, Cameroon, German South West Africa and German East Africa. Not only did these territories supply Germany with valuable mineral resources, but they also afforded ports on both the west and east coasts of Africa, which provided fuelling and maintenance facilities for German warships operating in the Atlantic and Indian Oceans.

The fighting in Africa was carried out almost exclusively by African colonial soldiers led by British, South African or German officers. Because the campaigns took place many thousands of miles from Europe, and involved virtually no European soldiers, they made little impact on those at home and were quickly forgotten afterwards. However, for anyone interested in early 20th century colonial history, the German campaigns in Africa during the Great War make a remarkable story. The four colonies were widely separated and the fighting which took place within the borders of each of them was very different. It is therefore impossible to recount the conduct of the four campaigns in such a brief description as this. Suffice it to say that each was cut off from the outside world on three sides by hostile territory, each was heavily outnumbered, and each was continually dogged by a severe shortage of all supplies (particularly medical). The German commanders must have been fully aware that they were fighting campaigns which could never be won. However, in the face of every difficulty, they conducted effective if unconventional operations which tied down very large British colonial forces. Above all, they inspired their African soldiers with the highest ideals of loyalty. For this reason alone, the campaigns are worthy of study.

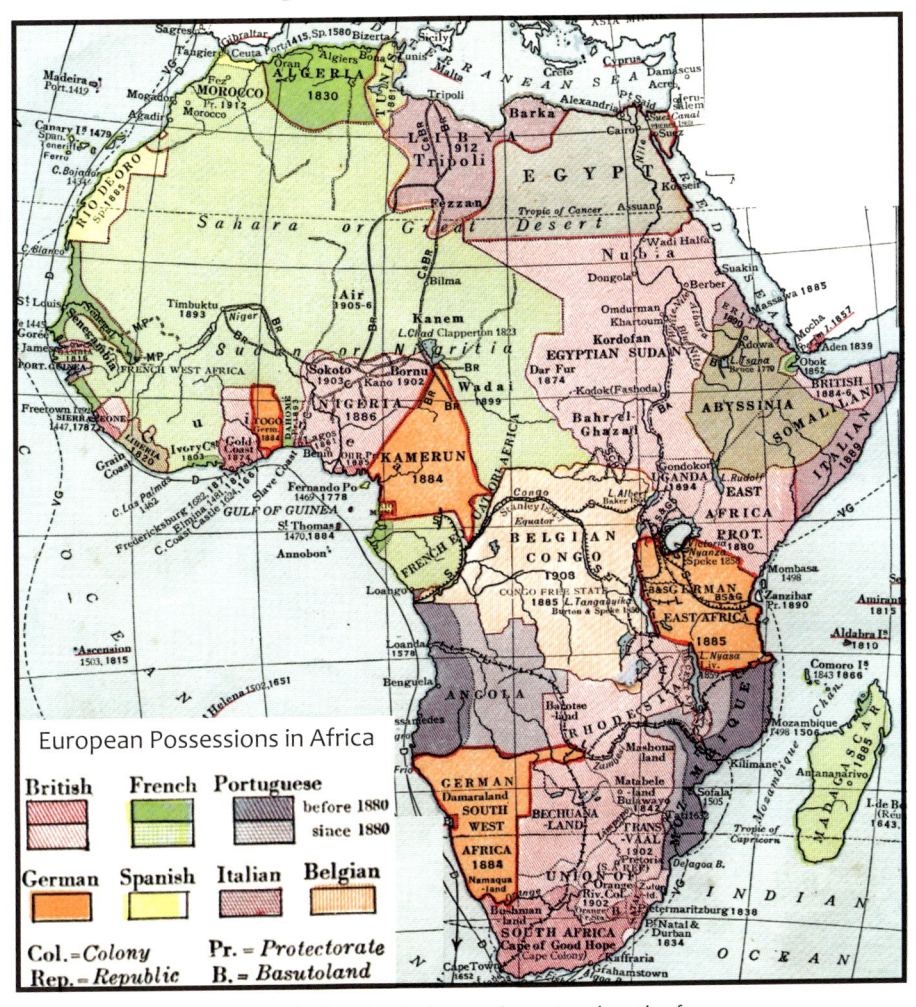

A map of Africa in the late 19th century has the four
German colonies coloured orange and outlined in red.

10: Medical History

In the South African War of 1899-1902, 20,000 British soldiers died, of whom only a quarter were killed by enemy action. In the Great War, 947,000 British soldiers died, of whom almost nine tenths were killed by enemy action. This radical proportional change can, of course, be largely explained by the increased intensity of the fighting; however, very great credit must be given to the Royal Army Medical Corps. In a nation such as Britain, where manpower potential was restricted, the maintenance of health was of vital importance throughout the war. The Field Service Regulations of 1912 laid down that the preservation of the health of troops was the primary function of the medical services. The subsequent rigid hygiene and sanitation discipline ensured a low sickness rate in soldiers. Although achieving this was may not have been the most exciting part of a doctor's work, it was vitally important.

The procedures for the treatment and evacuation of the wounded, in the setting of trench warfare, were developed and refined during the Great War. It was realised that the greatest factor in saving life was professional medical aid at the earliest opportunity, and thereafter quick evacuation from the battle area, where further medical attention could be given in comparative peace and quiet.

Every fighting unit had a Regimental Medical officer, who had a small team of stretcher bearers and medical orderlies whom he was required to train. In battle, his task was to establish a Regimental Aid Post, at a suitable distance behind the forward troops, to which casualties could either make their own way, or be carried by stretcher bearers. First aid or vital surgery was carried out in the Regimental Aid Post, before the casualty was despatched to the rear as quickly as possible. In practice, Regimental Medical Officers became convinced that lives would be lost unless they established their Regimental Aid Posts even further forward, often in shell holes, so that casualties could be treated with even great immediacy. Doctors and their dedicated staff of orderlies and stretcher bearers behaved with a courage that has probably never been matched in the history of war, and in doing so saved untold lives. Only three men have ever won a bar to the Victoria Cross and two of those three were in the Royal Army Medical Corps. Doctors and their staff wore prominent Red Cross armbands and, although there is no record of their ever being deliberately shot at by Germans, artillery shells are less selective; medical casualties were very high. During the war, about a thousand Regimental Medical Officers were killed in action. This represents a significant proportion of a skilled profession whose numbers could not be quickly replaced. In 1917, a Medical Commission reported that the supply of qualified doctors was critical and that Regimental Medical Officers must be restrained from what it described as 'acts of mistaken gallantry'. This edict seems to have had little effect.

When a man was evacuated from the battle area, he was transported first through an Advanced Dressing Station to a Casualty Clearing Station. As the war developed these became highly efficient emergency hospitals in which major surgery could be carried out under antiseptic conditions. Much of the nursing staff was female. As an example of the numbers that Casualty Clearing Stations could handle, it should be noted that stations in just one sector, that of the 4th Army, dealt with 14,400 wounded on the first day of the Battle of the Somme.

From the Casualty Clearing Stations, men were evacuated to Base Hospitals either in France or England. Such was the speed and efficiency of the medical evacuation chain that, by the latter stages of the war, a soldier could be between clean sheets in an English hospital twenty four hours after being wounded.

The critical shortage of doctors has already been mentioned. In April 1917, the difficulty of finding doctors meant that an urgent request was made to the USA for qualified Medical Officers. So generous was the resulting response that by June 1918 there were 1,200 American doctors serving with the British Army in France.

Their contribution was vital; not only did they augment the dwindling supply of British doctors but they brought with them medical advances in new technology. One example was the technique of blood transfusion which had been developed in the USA and was first used in Casualty Clearing Stations on the Western Front.

Thomas Rendle was a Bandsman, and therefore a stretcher bearer, with 1.DCLI at Wulverghem, in Belgium. He is shown (top) shortly after he was awarded the Victoria Cross for his action on 20th November 1914 and, below, as a bandmaster in later life.

It was not only physical damage for which men required attention. No consideration of medical treatment should omit a final word about that emotive subject: 'Shell Shock'.

The sheer intensity of battle, continued over long periods, was a new experience to all armies. Modern artillery could create catastrophic mayhem which literally drove men mad. All ranks in the army had been brought up in the hard school, accepting death and danger as one of the aspects of military life. However, even in the first months of the war when the army consisted entirely of seasoned regular soldiers, it became apparent that men could sometimes not stand up mentally to prolonged exposure to artillery. The immediate reaction by those of more robust temperament, and by those who had not experienced this new phenomenon was to brand 'shell shock' victims as cowards. Certain medical officers however, disagreed. Captain McMoron Wilson (later Lord Moran, the King's doctor) propounded a radical view which is now accepted teaching. In 'The Anatomy of Courage', he said that every man has a reserve of courage - some considerable, others minimal, but in every case finite. From the moment that a man is subjected to the terror of battle, that store of courage begins to leak away. Men with a smaller reserve of courage will crack up first, but every human being, regardless of his bravery, will eventually fail, unless taken right out of that environment. Caught in the early stages, the simple expedient of peace, rest and sleep could restore a man's courage and self respect. However, if left too late, a good and brave soldier could finish his days in a mental asylum, or even more tragically, in front of a firing squad and branded as a coward.

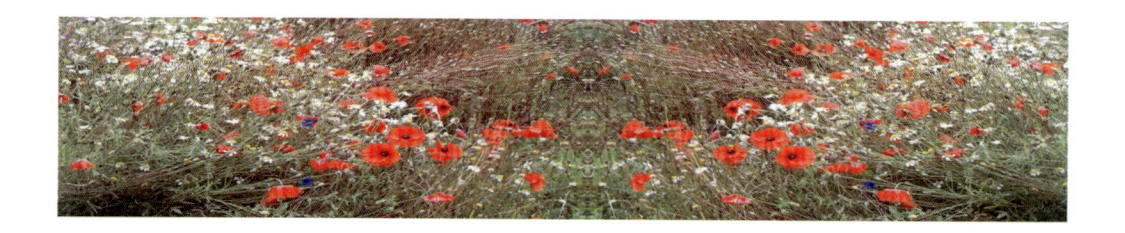

11: Executions

The execution of soldiers who had been found guilty of cowardice or desertion in the face of the enemy was highly controversial at the time, and, over eighty years later is still a subject of heated debate. Some offences listed in the Army Act had carried the death penalty long before the Great war, and still did so till the 1970s. However, since the latter part of the 19th century, the only time that the death sentence has been carried out was in the years between 1914 and 1918. Why was it thought necessary to impose such draconian measures during the Great War, particularly in view of the fact that up to 1916 every single soldier was a volunteer? This question has been argued from every point of view and there still seems to be no answer.

A French military execution, probably at Verdun in 1915

From the early days of the war, regimental officers, medical officers, padres and, indeed, the more enlightened senior officers, believed that the prolonged catastrophic noise and destruction of modern artillery fire was an entirely new phenomenon in war. Officers with considerable experience of past battles became convinced that a human being, regardless of his bravery, was often unable to retain his sanity under these conditions.

An overall judgement is made impossible because of the wide range of circumstances under which men were convicted. Some men deliberately hid themselves away when their battalions were due to go back into the line, often living with girls whom they had picked up during their rest period. This behaviour broke the very essence of a soldier's code of honour - that of shirking responsibility to your comrades and letting them down when they faced danger. Such men undoubtedly received little sympathy from the vast majority of soldiers, who stuck together with stolid courage and were prepared to meet their fate.

There were, however, many men who broke down in battle. Their minds could take no more and they were found huddled in the bottom of a trench, weeping or wandering about as if in a dream. It is very difficult indeed to put forward any justification for the conviction and execution of these poor sick souls, some of whom had previously displayed singular courage over a long period.

None of us was born in the latter years of the 19th century, and it is therefore impossible for us to put ourselves completely into the minds of the young men who fought in the Great War. They belonged to a robust but very disciplined generation which, at all levels of society, accepted authority, and were no strangers to severe punishment.

The use of the death penalty in the Great War will, arguably, always remain a tragic blot on the administration of discipline in the British Army. It cannot have been justified by the principle of "pour encourager les autres" because the others regularly faced death whenever they were in the line. The whole affair seems to have been viewed with embarrassed distaste - why else should these life or death Courts Martial have been conducted with such unseemly haste, without even a strict adherence to the legal procedures required by the Army Act of that time?

You must be left the judge of this unpalatable aspect of the Great War. Three hundred and six men were executed. Were these executions always justified? Were they ever justified? Should free pardons have been given to these long dead soldiers long before the debate of recent years?

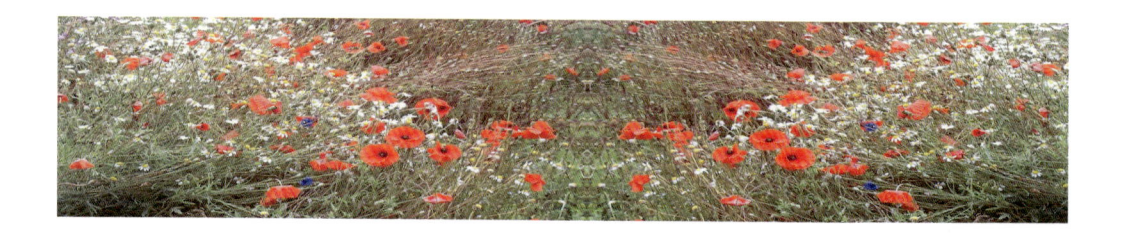

12: Religion

Whatever motivated the average British soldier of 1914-18, the Christian faith was of little significance. Britain was predominantly an urban society, whose working population seldom attended a church or knew anything of their parish priest (this was not true of the Roman Catholic and Methodist communities). The padres who saw active service in the first years of the war found themselves in a totally alien situation, in which they were incapable of forming any relationship with the soldiers. Indeed, this was one of the main factors which brought home to the Church its failure to communicate with the majority of the nation.

A padre gives water to a wounded soldier near Potijze in 1917. (Imperial War Museum)

The situation was not improved by the policy of forbidding padres to go into the front line, (for the reason that it would be bad for soldiers' morale to see 'men of God' killed or mutilated!) Almost every diary or memoir is deeply critical of padres who could only be found when a unit was at rest. Padres were naturally held in low esteem by those who bore the brunt of danger and discomfort in the forward trenches. This was especially sad as men, living amongst death in the front line, would have welcomed spiritual support.

After about 1916 there was a radical change, probably brought about by the padres themselves. Padres moved freely in the front line, and even 'went over the top' in attacks, ministering to the dying. A very large part of their job involved the burial of the dead. This was an operation, which by its terrible scale, could easily have degenerated into something inhuman and mechanical. Padres strove valiantly to try to ensure that every corpse was laid to rest with dignity.

Roman Catholic and Non-Conformists padres always seemed to have had a far closer rapport with their flock, a relationship on which many authors of the period comment.

The Great War represented a crisis point in the Anglican Church which was to result in great changes. At the beginning, padres were not only curtailed in their duties by official policy but were socially and intellectually incapable of forming any worthwhile relationship with the men. By the end of the war, this situation had changed radically for the better.

13: The Armistice

Although the Germans were in retreat by the Autumn of 1918, they still fought with considerable skill and determination. One has only got to look at the British casualty figures of this period to realise that for the soldier in the front line, the war was far from over. It was not only the fighting troops who could see little hope of immediate victory; as late as October 1918, the General Staff appreciation was that the British Army would have to hold on for another winter. A Spring offensive was planned for 1919, when the American forces would be more experienced and better trained. How was it then that in the early hours of 11th November, all front line units received the following signal?

'Hostilities will cease 1100 hours today November 11th. Troops will stand fast in line reached at that hour which will be reported by wire to Corps HQ.
Defensive precautions will be maintained. There will be no intercourse of any description with the enemy.'

During the fifty years before the Great War, the population of Germany had risen from 40 million to 76 million. A nation that had, in 1864, been capable of feeding itself, had, by 1914, become heavily reliant on imported food. When Germany went to war in 1914, she had reckoned on a swift and decisive victory; the problems of feeding her population over a protracted period did not concern her leaders.

The first action by the Royal Navy in August 1914 was to impose a blockade of all German ports. This tedious and unglamorous task was to prove the Royal Navy's critical role over the next four years, and the one which was to play a major part in bringing Germany to her knees.

Bread was rationed in Germany from January 1915, closely followed by meat, butter, tea, coffee, sugar and eggs. The grain harvests of 1916 and 1917 were exceptionally poor, and the winter of 1916-17 became known as 'turnip winter', due to the almost exclusive, unnourishing and monotonous diet. It is reckoned that a daily intake of 2,280 calories represents a bare subsistence level for a working man or woman; by 1918 the average daily intake of the German civilian was down to 1,000 calories. Quite apart from the very considerable increase in death resulting in disease brought on by cold and malnutrition, three quarters of a million German civilians died of starvation during the Great War. Food riots became increasingly common in many major towns. A Bolshevist movement, similar to that which had seized power in Russia gained ever greater strength. This was the home background that precipitated the German military collapse of October 1918.

The front page of the New York Times on November 11th, 1918

At the end of September 1918, Bulgaria had surrendered and Austro-Hungary was on the point of collapse. It was obvious to Von Ludendorff, the German Commander-in-Chief, that he would soon have to face a full scale allied offensive on his unprotected southern flank. On 3rd October, he persuaded his political leaders to approach President Wilson, of the USA, with a request for an armistice. This was immediately passed to the Prime Ministers of Great Britain and France, who happened to be meeting in London that day.

It must be emphasised at this point that a request for an armistice was not a surrender. An armistice was traditionally only a temporary cessation of hostilities, negotiated between the opposing generals, to allow the politicians to discuss a more permanent peace settlement. The armistice of November 1918, however, was unique. Because of the vast complexity of the war itself, the generals were playing a far greater role, not just on the battlefield, but in the overall control of their respective nations. Thus the armistice, which had traditionally been the province of the generals, became in effect a peace treaty negotiated largely by the generals and not by the politicians.

From the outset, Haig eagerly grasped the opportunity to achieve peace. Those who brand him as a butcher would do well to read his impassioned pleas to end the slaughter. Furthermore, the allied offensive of 1918 had been largely carried out by British and Commonwealth troops, and Haig saw no reason why his men should continue to die for a cause which they had already won.

The war had been fought on French soil, and France had suffered far higher casualties than Britain. It is not therefore surprising that Marshall Foch, the French Commander-in-Chief should have insisted on a harder bargain in his negotiations. Foch and Haig had born the burden of war together, and were united in their belief that this tentative hope of peace must be exploited. On the last day of October 1918, Foch was asked whether it was better to accept the armistice or to continue the war to its ultimate conclusion, when Germany must submit to unconditional surrender. He replied:

'I do not make war for the purpose of making war but for the purpose of getting results. If the Germans sign an armistice with the conditions recognised as necessary to guarantee to us the results, I am satisfied. No one has the right to prolong the bloodshed longer.'

The American reaction was, to say the least, startling. General Pershing, the United States Commander-in-Chief, delivered a note to the Allied leaders on 30th October, in which he opposed granting an armistice at all. His motives are obscure. Pershing was not a subtle man, but an unimaginative plodder of little intellectual ability. It is therefore difficult to attribute to him the Machiavellian motives ascribed to him in his handling of the proposed armistice. However, like many Americans, he tended to see the war as a means for the United States to make its mark in world affairs. Furthermore, he himself had growing aspirations to the Presidency and was fully aware that, previously, every American war had propelled a successful general into that supreme position. Pershing undoubtedly disliked Wilson and, it is believed, could have gone to considerable lengths to discredit Wilson's armistice negotiations. This would have been a matter of deep disloyalty on Pershing's part for, in the United States, the President is the Commander-in-Chief of all American Forces. Wilson was therefore Pershing's direct military superior. The second reason put forward for Pershing's opposition to an armistice was even more repellent. If he was to succeed to the Presidency, he must be seen as a successful general. This he was not; his troops were still learning their trade in France and had not been involved in a single major battle. If the war could be continued through the winter, the Americans would play a decisive role in the final offensive planned for Spring 1919. Pershing's reasons for opposing the armistice have never been fully established, but the fact that he did oppose it did neither him nor the United States any credit in the eyes of Britain and France. His note of 30th October was ignored.

The terms of the armistice signed on 11th November 1918 were largely drafted by Foch. The fact that the document imposed such punitive terms on Germany is understandable but these punitive terms undoubtedly led to the eventual rise of the National Socialist party and thus to the Second World War.

A famous illustration by an unknown artist shows the signing of the armistice in the personal railway carriage of Maréchal Foch, who is standing behind the table. The painting is inaccurate as regards furniture and other details.

From left to right the figures are:
German Admiral Ernst Vanselow, German Count Alfred von Oberndorff of the Foreign Ministry, German army general Detlof von Winterfeldt (in helmet), British Royal Navy Captain Jack Marriott (Naval Assistant to the First Sea Lord), Matthias Erzberger, head of the German delegation, British Rear-Admiral George Hope (Deputy First Sea Lord), British Admiral of the Fleet Sir Rosslyn Wemyss (First Sea Lord), Marshal of France Ferdinand Foch, and French general Maxime Weygand.

The harsh terms and the use of the carriage were long and bitterly remembered in Germany. When an armistice was imposed on France on 22 June 1940, the same carriage (which had been preserved with a plaque reading: *'Here, on 11th November 1918, succumbed the criminal pride of the German Reich, vanquished by the free peoples which it tried to enslave'*), was removed to Compiegne, where the armistice of 1918 had been signed. Hitler then sat in the same chair in which Marshal Ferdinand Foch had sat in 1918, but in an intentional act of disdain left as soon as the premable to the treaty was read.

14: The Treaty of Versailles

The Treaty of Versailles, the document which officially brought peace to the warring nations, was signed on 28th June 1919.

The Treaty has fifteen parts, covers hundreds of pages and is extremely complicated. No attempt is made here to cover it in detail, but the essence of the six most important parts (I, II, III, IV, V and VIII) is outlined below.

Part I provided for the formation of the League of Nations. This was a body formed with the intention of ensuring the integrity of all nation states against armed agression. It laid down strict rules for the reduction of armaments and for the close supervision of the arms trade with backward countries. Significantly, the United States of America did not sign Part I and was therefore excluded from much of the subsequent negotiations.

Parts II and III dealt with the redistribution of former German territory. This can be summed up as follows:

The frontier districts of Moresnet, Eupen and Malmedy were transferred to Belgium. The rich mining area of the Saar was placed in the control of the League, whilst its coal mines were ceded to France. Alsace and Lorraine were transferred to France. The Rhineland was declared a demilitarised area. Schleswig was transferred to Denmark. West Prussia and most of Posnan then became part of a re-established Poland (thus effectively splitting Germany in two halves to East and West of the so called 'Danzig Corridor')

In all, Germany forfeited about 25,000 square miles, lost a population of about 6 million, and was deprived of a large part of her mineral resources (65% of iron, 45% of coal, 72% of zinc and 57% of lead).

Part IV stripped Germany of all her overseas colonies.

Part V dealt with the virtual disarmament of Germany.
Her army was to be reduced to a home defence force of no more than 100,000 men. Artillery, tanks and munitions were to be reduced to a corresponding level. Conscription was forbidden. The manufacture of munitions was to be supervised by the League and the import of munitions forbidden.

The German navy was to be severely scaled down. The German airforce was to be disbanded. Every existing military aircraft was to be destroyed and the future manufacture of military aircraft or air munitions forbidden.

Part VIII, possibly the most important and far reaching section, dealt with the reparations which Germany was required to pay. There was sharp disagreement amongst the Allies as to how much Germany could realistically be expected to produce. British experts tended to favour a total of about £2,000 million. A special Reparations Committee had been previously set up, consisting of permanent members from the USA, France, Great Britain and Italy (with an additional member from Belgium, Yugoslavia or Japan being co-opted, if the particular matter under discussion affected one of these countries). The failure of the USA to ratify Part I of the Treaty rendered them ineligible to sit on the Reparations Committee, which reduced it to three permanent members. France, as the nation which had suffered the greatest devastation, presided and had the casting vote. Thus France and Belgium were able to outvote Great Britain and Italy, and often did. The final decision by the Committee was that Germany should be charged reparations to the value of £8,200 million (over four times the figure submitted by the British). Germany was quite incapable of meeting the debt in cash, and most was eventually paid in kind, which included ships, railway materials, coal, building materials and livestock.

Implications of the Treaty

The Treaty of Versailles was most bitterly resented by the German people. It had not merely been dictated by the victors to the vanquished (which is indeed the usual result of war), but Germany had been given no opportunity to enter into any verbal negotiations concerning its implementation. This was unprecedented in the history of modern politics, and it must further be remembered that Germany had not surrendered in 1918 (as she was to do in 1945) but had merely agreed to an armistice.

The final reparations imposed on Germany (largely against the advice of Great Britain) were to lead to hyper-inflation, starvation, the collapse of legitimate government, the power struggle between militant communist and national socialist splinter groups, and the emergence of the Nazi party.

Furthermore, Germany had been made to feel bitterly humiliated by the breaking up of her nation into the Reich and East Prussia, separated by the Polish 'Danzig Corridor'. The German States had been united by Bismarck in 1871 and Germans had felt very deeply about their new-found nationhood. This was a final and devastating blow to their pride.

The Treaty of Versailles was devised by the victorious powers, without consultation with the vanquished. It imposed draconian terms which, in the long term, proved impossible to implement. It was not so much a peace treaty as a design for the deliberate crushing of a nation which was perceived as the perpetrator of the most devastating war in history.

We now know that it imposed economic demands which could never be paid, territorial forfeitures which could never be accepted, and that it drove a humiliated nation to desperate measures. We are right to subject the Treaty to the severest criticism, but we do so with hindsight. The diplomats, politicians and soldiers who formulated the Treaty in 1919 had just lived through four years of mayhem which had threatened the very foundations of European civilisation. The victors (particularly France) hated Germany and were absolutely determined she should never again be capable of military action. They might possibly have succeeded, were it not that the League of Nations (not unlike the United Nations) had no teeth and was unable to enforce the measures that it had decreed.

Today, we know how the measures promulgated by the Treaty of Versailles led inexorably to the Second World War. But that, as they say, is another story.

LEAGUE OF NATIONS

SOCIETE DES NATIONS

The later logo of the League of Nations, the organisation which attempted to prevent further conflict between nations, but failed.

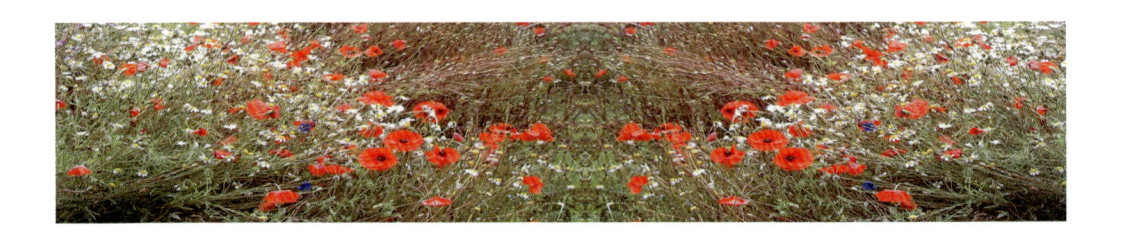

15: Conclusion

Casualties

Our enduring memory of the Great War is undoubtedly that of the human slaughter. The death toll was in fact considerably less than that of the Second World War, but the fact that much of the killing took place within a narrow strip of land, running from the North Sea to Switzerland, provides us with a mental picture of unique horror. This front, on which most British soldiers fought, was known as the Western Front; it must, however, never be forgotten that, as in the Second World War, there was also an Eastern Front, in which the bloody intensity of the fighting left a death toll in the Russian Army which has never been accurately assessed.

The following figures of dead are rounded to the nearest thousand. Within this bracket they are probably reasonably accurate, though those of Russia most certainly represent an under-estimate.

Allied Powers
- Russia — 1,700,000 (but probably more)
- France — 1,400,000
- Great Britain — 947,000
- Italy — 660,000
- British Dominions and Colonies — 659,000
- USA — 116,000
- Belgium — 14,000

5,496,000

Central Powers
- Germany — 1,800,000
- Austro Hungarian Empire — 1,200,000
- Ottoman Empire (mainly Turkey) — 325,000

3,325,000

The total for deaths in the populations of those nations which played a major role in the war therefore comes to a total of 8,821,000

To this figure should be added the death toll of the several nations who were only marginally involved.

It is impossible to give the final total of deaths arising from the conflict, but in all, it cannot have been far short of 10 million people.

To belittle the loss of nearly a million British soldiers would be a gross insult to their widows and families; nevertheless, these figures should be examined with great care. It has become one of the myths of our accepted history that Britain suffered a disproportionate toll of death in the Great War, and that this was responsible for her subsequent decline as a world power. British losses were indeed appalling but they were light in comparison to those of France and Germany as the following figures demonstrate.

Country	Population	Number Killed	Percentage
France	38,000,000	1,400,000	3.68%
Germany	65,000,000	1,800,000	2.76%
Great Britain	50,000,000	947,000	1.89%

These percentages may not immediately appear catastrophic but, when one considers that approximately half of any population were females, and, of the males, only about a third were of the age group which was eligible for service, the picture is dramatically changed.

For every hundred men who served in the armed forces France lost 22 men, Germany 17 men and Great Britain 11 men.

In Britain, we tend to harbour an arrogant and derogatory opinion about the fighting spirit of France, suggesting that we have always had to go to war in order to bail her out. The casualty figures should speak for themselves. The French bore the brunt of the fighting on the Western Front and their army suffered the most appalling losses which have seldom, if ever, been equalled in history. To the human carnage must be added the total destruction of hundreds of French towns and villages within the fighting area, and the degradation suffered by that part of their population which lived in areas occupied by the German Army. All this goes a long way to explain French military, political and social history in the years since 1918.

Great Britain's loss of 947,000 men was, however, of extra significance to our Nation. Unique within Europe, the British Army had no conscription until 1916. Every single British serviceman before that was a volunteer, and those that answered the call to arms did so out of a deep sense of duty and pride. They exchanged secure jobs and comfortable domesticity for the spartan conditions of makeshift training camps. They carried their pride, courage and humour to the battlefields of the Western Front, where a high proportion were killed or mutilated. These were the cream of British manhood; their deaths represented an irreplaceable loss to our Nation.

Social Change

One has only to look at photographs of people taken immediately before and after the Great War, to realise that a dramatic social change took place during those four years. Pre 1914 scenes show a world little changed from the latter days of Queen Victoria's reign, whilst those of post 1918 depict a way of life that is immediately recognisable to modern eyes. It is said that the visible signs of social change are usually most apparent in women's fashions. Certainly the woman of 1914 in her long skirt revealing the merest glimpse of a booted ankle and her large 'cartwheel' hat could not have provided a stranger contrast to her appearance four years later in a skirt worn well above the knee, bobbed hair and cloche hat.

The driving force of change certainly appears to have been provided by women. Before 1914, the employment of women was generally confined to domestic service and work in the textile mills, while the vast majority of women remained at home, cooking, cleaning and bringing up their children. Women had little, if any, financial independence, and even those in employment received wages far lower than those paid to men.

In the latter part of 1914, an unprecedented number of men left their jobs to enlist in the armed forces. By the beginning of 1916, conscription was introduced, further draining the Nation's civilian resources.

Women, of necessity, quickly filled the gaps. As far as is known, women were never employed in the coal mines, the heaviest industries or on the railways, but they played a full part in almost every other occupation. In particular, the enormous expansion of the munitions industry, and the requirement not only to maintain, but to increase, agricultural production, provided work for hundreds of thousands of women. Pay, certainly in the munition factories, was good; for the first time, a significant proportion of women became financially independent, no longer relying on what their husbands might care to hand over each Friday night. Having tasted this new found freedom, they were never to return to a world in which they were totally subservient to men.

At the same time, the mud and blood of the Western Front was having a profound effect on men. Never before had all classes lived cheek by jowl in such conditions of discomfort and danger. Shells and bullets do not discriminate between rank, and the rain falls with equal wetness on the colonel and the private.

Intense bonds of comradeship were forged in the filth and misery of those battlefields, and a relationship developed between officers and soldiers

Women were transformed by the need for them to work in roles which had traditionally been seen as the preserve of men and by the changes this then wrought on their social position and their own outlook.

These pictures of two groups, one of a family in 1913 and the other from the 1920s, emphasise the changes arising over just ten years in fashion, attitude and social interaction. The number of women in the lower picture could be an indication of the problems arising from the high death toll of the war.

which was a new phenomenon. The military hierarchy was always maintained, but it was transcended by a spirit of deep understanding between ranks. Officers came to know their soldiers at a much deeper level and to appreciate their robustness, courage, aspirations and fears. Soldiers, living so close to their officers, also came to appreciate the lonely demands of leadership and responsibility. The comradeship between all ranks in a good platoon became such a powerful force that it can only be described as love. This love becomes very evident when one reads surviving letters from young officers to the mothers and widows of dead soldiers. Often written in pencil on pages torn from a field service note book, they evoke not just formal sympathy, but a genuine feeling of desolation for a dead comrade. It was this love that drove officers to acts of reckless bravery to rescue wounded soldiers, and soldiers to perform similar acts to bring in their officers.

The old pre-1914 relationships could never be re-established when the army was demobilised after the war. How could men who had experienced such awesome events return to a society that was perceived to be irrelevant.

In Kipling's words:
>
> Me that 'ave been what I've been -
> Me that 'ave gone where I've gone -
> Me that 'ave seen what I've seen -
> 'Ow can I ever take on
> With awful old England again,
> And 'ouses both sides of the street,
> And 'edges two sides of the lane,
> And the parson an' gentry between,
> An' touchin' my 'at when we meet -
> Me that 'ave been what I've been?

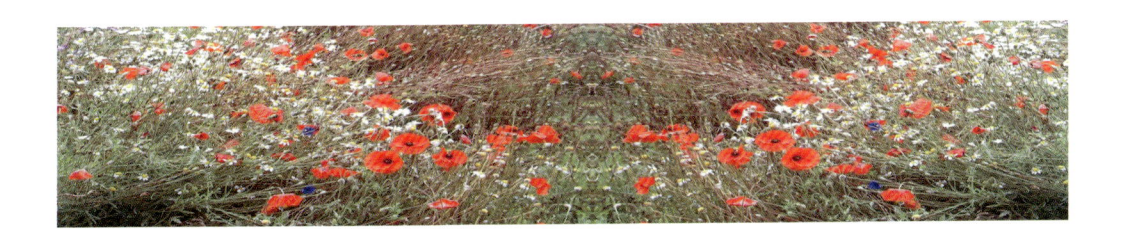

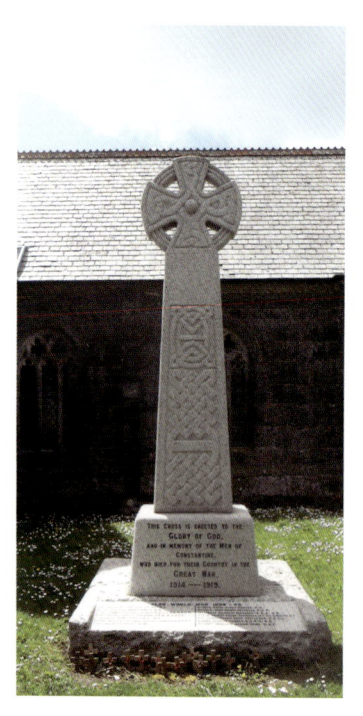

Two memorials erected near a Parish Church are typical of those found throughout the country.
Left: Constantine, Cornwall.   Right: Tywardreath, Cornwall.

    The dead of the Great War are still remembered by the 'war memorials' which were erected in almost every parish and carry the engraved names of those who died. These memorials, usually funded by public subscription, were erected in honour, a word now often overlooked, of those of the village who fell in the Great War. The memorials vary from the simple to the grand, but were always erected with care and skillful carving and the names of the fallen engraved on stone or slate. Today, they remain the focus of annual celebration in memory of the dead and of the attempt 'to end all wars'. Abroad, they are complemented by the fields of simple white crosses in memory of the fallen. These memorials are spread across the battlefields of France and Belgium and are a continuing and surviving wonder.

    These memorials, erected immediately after the end of the war, were intended to ensure that the lives of the fallen should not be forgotten, and as a reminder that such conflict should be avoided. They remain a continuing memorial to the conflict and to that human experience.

This example of a memorial is in the tiny Parish of Boconnoc, Cornwall.
Photograph: Clare Fortescue

One of the most beautiful and inspring of all memorials is that at Winchester, where the long roll of dead young school leavers is engraved around a cloister.

The Organisation of the British Infantry in the First World War

This diagram lays out a plan of the organisation that might have been found in 1914.

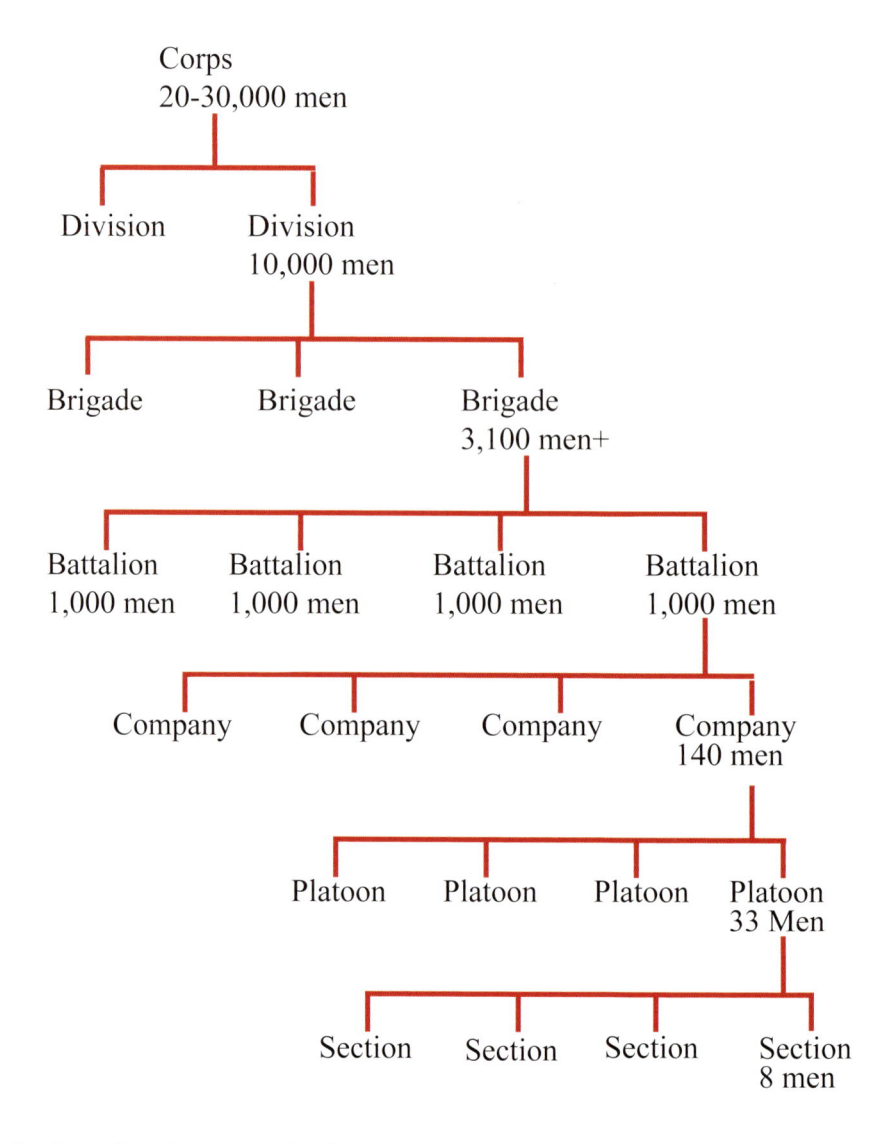

```
Corps
20-30,000 men
├── Division
└── Division
    10,000 men
    ├── Brigade
    ├── Brigade
    └── Brigade
        3,100 men+
        ├── Battalion 1,000 men
        ├── Battalion 1,000 men
        ├── Battalion 1,000 men
        └── Battalion 1,000 men
            ├── Company
            ├── Company
            ├── Company
            └── Company
                140 men
                ├── Platoon
                ├── Platoon
                ├── Platoon
                └── Platoon
                    33 Men
                    ├── Section
                    ├── Section
                    ├── Section
                    └── Section
                        8 men
```

The Words 'Army' or 'Formation' referred to groups or bodies of men without specific definition and could refer to groupings of any size.
The Word 'Regiment' referred to the recruiting base and grouping of men in a battalion.
Men from different regiments could form part of any group from a Battalion upwards.
The groups of men in artilliery, staff, engineering, medical services, or in the observer, supply or other ancillary corps are not included in the organisation chart above.
Territorial and Colonial armies also had a different organisation.
The chart does not reflect the changes in operation and command structure that arose during the progress of the war.

Appendix 1:
The Organisation of the British Army

BATTALION

In the British Army, this was normally a unit of infantry commanded by a Lieutenant Colonel. The official war establishment was 30 officers and 977 other ranks, giving a total of 1,007 all ranks. However, with the continual attrition of war, battalions usually operated at well below this establishment figure. The essential fighting element of a battalion was its four companies, each consisting of 6 officers and 140 other ranks, commanded by a Captain. A Company was divided into four platoons, each commanded by a Lieutenant or Second Lieutenant, and a platoon was divided into four sections each commanded by a Corporal. Previous to 1913, a battalion had had eight companies. Although all regular battalions went to war in 1914 with the four company establishment described above, many Territorial Force battalions were still organised under the old eight company system.

Like all British military nomenclature, the word 'battalion' can be misleading. British units were described as battalions, and most foreign or American units, of whatever arm, were also described as battalions.

Apart from the battalions that fought in the front line, there were also a very large number of training and reserve battalions based in Britain. These, as their name suggests, had the role of training recruits and holding drafts ready for posting abroad as and when required.

BRIGADE

Commanded by a Brigadier-General. There were three infantry brigades to a division. Up to February 1918, a brigade consisted of four battalions with a total strength of 372 officers and 11,793 other ranks. It was the smallest formation that was self-contained with units of artillery, engineers, signals and supporting services. By the end of 1917 it had become obvious that Britain was running out of manpower and that it would be necessary to make cuts. Against military advice this was achieved by cutting a brigade from four to three battalions, which meant that the regimental officers and soldiers spent a higher proportion of their time in the front line.

COMPANY

A company was normally a fourth part of the fighting establishment of an infantry battalion. Its official strength varied at different periods of the war, due to the widespread introduction of specialist weapons like the Lewis light machine-gun but was always around 140 all ranks. This figure was often appreciably lower due to attrition of war. A company was commanded by a Captain. There was usually another Captain or a Lieutenant as the second-in-command, and a Lieutenant or Second Lieutenant in command of each of the four platoons.

The term 'company' was also used by the Royal Engineers. These companies differed widely according to their particular specialist role.

CORPS
A corps, commanded by a Lieutenant General, had at least two divisions.

DIVISION
Commanded by a Major-General. This fighting formation, made up of three, sometimes four brigades, formed the basis for all high command tactics. It was also the largest formation which, generally speaking, retained its composition intact throughout the war. Battalions which formed part of a particular division in 1914 were usually still with that division four years later. Consequently, a certain esprit de corps became established. The total war establishment of a division was 18,073 all ranks.

FORMATION
A word used in the British Army to describe any grouping of all arms, that is to say a brigade, division, corps or army.

PLATOON
Normally a fourth part of the fighting establishment of an infantry company. Its official strength varied at different periods of the war, due to the introduction of specialist weapons, but was always around 33 all ranks. This figure was often appreciably lower due to the attrition of war. A platoon should have been commanded by a Lieutenant or Second Lieutenant. However, because the casualty rate amongst junior officers was extremely high and replacements of sufficient quality difficult to find as the war dragged on, platoons were therefore often commanded by Serjeants or even Corporals.

RANKS
Field-Marshal - The highest rank in the British Army. In 1914, there were only two Field Marshals on the active list.

General - Commanded an army of at least two corps. All officers could also hold staff appointments.

Lieutenant-General - Commanded a corps of at least two divisions.

Major-General - Commanded a division of four brigades. It is typical of British Army logic that a Major-General should be junior to a Lieutenant-General.

Brigadier-General - Commanded a brigade of four battalions (three battalions after February 1918).

Colonel - Normally a staff appointment only.

Lieutenant-Colonel - Commanded a major unit, that is to say a regiment of artillery, a regiment of cavalry, a signals regiment, tank battalion or, most commonly, an infantry battalion.

Major - At the start of the war in 1914, there were normally two majors in a unit. One acted as Second-in-Command, responsible for much of the day to day administration and smooth running of the unit, whether in or out of action. As far as possible, he was kept out of danger in battle, so that he could go forward and take over should his Commanding Officer be killed or wounded.

Captain - Commanded a battery of artillery, squadron of cavalry, tank company, infantry company or any of the many 'minor units' of supporting services.

Lieutenant and Second Lieutenant - Known as 'subalterns'. Commanded a platoon or equivalent. Subalterns were always in short supply - first, because there was never sufficient good, young material available; secondly, because their casualty rate was extremely high and exceeded the rate that they could be produced by the officer training schools.

Adjutant - This was an appointment, and not a rank, which was usually held by a Lieutenant or Captain. He was the Commanding Officer's right hand man, and was responsible to him for every aspect of staff work within the unit which affected operations or personnel. He drafted most orders and dealt with the correspondence emanating from the headquarters, and was responsible for the discipline of the unit. His workload was daunting, but the delegation of such power to a young officer provided the very best training for future command.

Quartermaster - This, again, was an appointment and not a rank. In 1914, most Quartermasters were normally Lieutenants, who had invariably been commissioned from the ranks. A quartermaster was responsible for every material need of the soldier, from socks to barrack accommodation, from food to louse powder, and for the requisitioning and allocation of billets when his unit was out of the line. A good Quartermaster could somehow conjure up a hot meal for the soldiers under the most diabolical conditions. He could scrounge extra stores or clothing, and appropriate the best billets for the unit when it came out of the line. In short, the morale and efficiency of a unit, particularly when times were hard, depended on the experience, ingenuity and determination of its Quartermaster.

Regimental Serjeant Major - Strictly speaking, this was an appointment and not a rank (the rank being Warrant Officer Class I). The Regimental Serjeant Major was undoubtedly the man who would have been best known to NCOs and soldiers, being responsible for their discipline. He exercised his considerable authority by sheer force of character, and was generally approached with some trepidation. His duties included the drawing and supply of ammunition, during both peace and war. Many Regimental Serjeant Majors performed acts of great gallantry leading ammunition parties forward under heavy fire.

Company Serjeant Major - Again, this was considered as an appointment and not a rank (the rank was Warrant Officer Class II). The Company Serjeant Major (or his equivalent) played the same role at sub-level as the Regimental Serjeant Major did at unit level.

Regimental Quartermaster Serjeant - He was the Quartermaster's right hand man.

Colour Serjeant - A Company or equivalent Quartermaster Serjeant who was responsible to his Company Commander.

Serjeant - Widely considered to be the backbone of the army. In the initial stages of the war, serjeants were highly experienced soldiers, who had been groomed in peacetime to accept responsibility far above their rank. A young subaltern and his serjeant formed an extremely close team.

Corporal or Lance Corporal - Commanded a section or equivalent, which was the bed-rock on which the morale and fighting spirit of a unit was built. The members of a good section lived, worked, played, groused and laughed together. They were 'mates' who knew each other so well that a bond of loyalty was developed which transcended the personal terrors and exhaustion of battle. In fostering this spirit, the humble Corporals and Lance Corporals played an absolutely vital role in ensuring that the foundations of this unit were strong and solid.

Private - The ancient tile accorded to the majority of those holding the lowest rank in the cavalry and infantry. Privates of the Royal Artillery were known as Gunners, privates of the Royal Engineers are known as Sappers and privates in the Rifle Regiments are known as Riflemen.

REGIMENT

A regiment is a complex formation and a word whose use must have confused enemy intelligence officers.

The basic unit of artillery, cavalry, engineers or signals in the British Army was, and still is, known as a regiment and is under a Lieutenant Colonel's command.

In the infantry the term has a quite different meaning. Every officer and soldier in the infantry belongs to a regiment. He wears a cap badge peculiar to that regiment and remains part of his regiment, quite regardless of where or in what capacity he is serving. To the infantryman, the regiment is his family, and, like every family, it has its own customs, traditions and idiosyncrasies. In one respect, all regiments are the same - they engender an immense spirit of pride which imbues soldiers with a determination to maintain the very highest standards, both in peace and war. The British regimental system, unique in Western armies, has undoubtedly been a significant factor in producing an army whose reputation stands second to none.

Infantry regiments (apart from the Brigade of Guards, the King's Royal Rifle Corps and the Rifle Brigade) were closely associated with those counties or areas of Britain from which they normally drew their recruits. These associations were usually reflected in the title of the regiment. Before 1914, regiments might have had five battalions. These comprised two regular battalions (one at home and one abroad), at least two Territorial Force battalions, at least one Militia Reserve battalion and a depot. This depot was invariably situated in the county or area with which the regiment was associated. All recruits were trained at the depot; it was the home of the regiment and formed a base from which regimental business was conducted.

SECTION

The fourth part of a platoon and the smallest sub unit of infantry. It consisted of about ten men commanded by a Corporal, with a Lance Corporal as his second-in-command. After 1915, a Lewis light machine-gun was introduced into each section, which gave enormously increased firepower. A good infantry section was an extremely tight knit group. It members lived, slept and endured danger and discomfort together, every man relying on the loyalty, robust humour, kindness and courage of his comrades. The humble section was the solid rock on which the whole fighting strength of an infantry battalion depended.

Appendix 2
Glossary and Biographies

ALSACE-LORRAINE
The territories forming the extreme eastern part of France along the Franco-German border, were ceded to Prussia after her victory against France in 1871. Alsace-Lorraine was ceded back to France in 1919 under the terms of the Treaty of Versailles.

ARMAGEDDON
The name given to the last mythical battle between good and evil before the final Day of Judgement.

BISMARCK, Otto von
Born in 1815. After a hell-raising youth, typical of the Prussian military aristocracy, Bismarck matured into one of the most powerful statesmen of 19th Century Europe who believed that political change could never be achieved by democratic means but by 'Iron and Blood'. Not only did Bismarck unite the small German states into a single nation, but, by military action, he ensured that this new nation dominated Europe. He achieved this latter aim by the systematic conquest of Denmark, Austria, and France.

BOSCHE
A derogatory slang term for a German.

CHATEAU
A French country house.

CHURCHILL, WINSTON, 1874-1966
Saw active service as a young man both as a cavalry officer and as a war correspondent before entering politics as a Liberal in 1900. He was appointed First Lord of the Admiralty in 1911 with the explicit task of 'putting the fleet into a state of instant readiness for war' and was the architect of the naval expedition to relieve Antwerp and of the Dardanelles campaign. Both of these operations proved failures but, had they succeeded, would have had a profound influence on the subsequent conduct of the war. Churchill was to lead the Nation in the Second World War as Prime Minister.

CONGRESS OF VIENNA, 1814-15
The Congress was convened in September 1814, merely to ratify the decisions signed by Britain, Austria, Prussia and Russia in the Treaty of Paris, which followed the initial fall of Napoleon. The Congress of Vienna became a glittering social gathering which brought together the principal statesmen of Europe. However, the congress also produced meticulous work which stood the test of time for the next forty years.

DANZIG

A Baltic port close to the mouth of the Vistula river. Under the Treaty of Versailles of 1919, Danzig and its surrounding territory were confiscated from Germany and declared a protectorate of the newly-founded League of Nations. This loss not only deprived Germany of an important port, but, together with the granting of the previous German states of West Prussia and Posnan, which were given to Poland, divided the former united Germany into separate parts. The so called Danzig corridor was bitterly resented by Germany. The reconquest of these territories in 1939 was the action that finally sparked off the Second World War.

FIELD GUN

A mobile gun capable of being towed, complete with its ammunition limber, by a team of six horses over all but the very worst ground.

FIRE AND MANOEUVRE

A system of moving when in contact with an enemy. The commander splits his troops into two groups. At any one time, one group is firmly static on the ground, thus providing covering fire while the other group moves. At no time are both groups on the move together.

FOCH, Ferdinand, Marshal of France 1851-1929

An officer of outstanding intelligence. He was Supreme Commander-in-Chief of the Allied Armies in France from March 1918.

FRANCO - PRUSSIAN WAR, 1870

This was the third and most traumatic of Bismarck's three wars of aggression and took place against Denmark, Austria and France. It was designed to promote Prussia as a leading nation in Europe. The humiliating defeat of France had the most profound echoes. Revolution erupted on 18th November 1871, when Paris was taken over by 'Les Communards'. After bitter fighting, French government troops eventually reasserted their authority. The revolution was finally crushed on 28th April 1871, in an orgy of killing. Government troops massacred 20,000 men, women and children. More Parisians died during this final bloody week than had died during the whole course of the more famous Revolution of 1798. The legacy of the war poisoned all relationships between France and Germany, and it is only now, after two further wars, that a fragile alliance is again being established.

FRENCH, Field Marshal Sir John, 1852-1925

Although brought up in England, French was of Norman-Irish stock and invariably described himself as an Irishman. In 1868, he joined the Royal Navy as a Cadet but, finding life at sea uncongenial, resigned two years later. Then, after passing out of the Royal Military College, Sandhurst in 1874, he was commissioned into the 8th Queen's Royal Hussars, transferring almost immediately to the 19th Hussars (a less expensive regiment). From his first days as a subaltern, he queried accepted military procedures and particularly the inward looking ethos of regimental officers. He never attended the Staff College, holding an implacable belief that any officer with sound regimental experience was better qualified to hold a staff appointment than one who had merely spent a couple of years at Camberley. In the South African War of 1899-1902 he commanded the cavalry and, by his dash and imagination, was largely responsible for the successful relief of Ladysmith.

In March 1914, French, as Chief of the Imperial General Staff, was caught up in what was to become known as the 'Curragh Mutiny'. The Ulster Unionists, refusing to be coerced into Home Rule, threatened armed resistance against the British, and raised a 100,000 strong, comparatively well-armed, secret army. The army at the Curragh was put under orders to stand by to carry out military operations against this force. A high proportion of the British officers either came from Ireland or were of Irish extraction. Many, like French, considered themselves more Irish than British, which put them under an intolerable conflict of loyalty - none more so than the Chief of the Imperial General Staff, who was forced to resign.

Appointed Commander-in-Chief of the British Expeditionary Force to France in August 1914, French had the unenviable job of leading a small British Army against vastly superior odds, whilst ensuring its survival. His xenophobic character did not help him in this, but there is no doubt that he was put in a near impossible situation.

French was a controversial and complex man, who inspired both intense loyalty and hatred. He was a highly professional soldier who twice in his career, (The Curragh Mutiny and command of the BEF) was confronted with insuperable problems. He could exhibit a violent temper and was known as a womaniser. Right up to his death, in 1925, his reputation was hotly disputed by military factions.

GORGETS

Originally a piece of throat armour this came to mean in modern times the pieces of coloured cloth worn on the collars of staff and senior officers.

GUERRILLA

A participant in a type of war waged against an occupying regular army by the employment of a force of loosely organised civilians, operating on their own home ground. Guerrillas seldom wear any form of uniform. Because they can melt away into the local population, and because they know the countryside better than the occupying forces, they can exert an influence out of all proportion to their numerical strength.

HAIG, Douglas Field-Marshal Earl, 1861-1928

Son of a whisky distiller. Unlike most of his contemporaries, Haig went up to Oxford to read for a degree before turning his attention to a military career. Commissioned into the 7th Hussars in 1885, he quickly made a name for himself as a serious, competent and highly professional soldier. During leave in the year 1895, he spent six months with the Germany Army, an attachment that gave him a unique insight into their modus operandi. After attending the Staff College in 1896, he saw active service with the Egyptian cavalry during the Nile Campaign of 1899, which afforded him an opportunity to test many of his radical, but carefully thought out innovations. In 1900, he was Chief-of-Staff to Major-General John French who commanded the Cavalry Division in South Africa, and, as a result of these experiences, chaired the committee with the task of pushing through a comprehensive reform of British cavalry.

In 1914, Haig accompanied the British Expeditionary Force to France, as Commander of 1st Corps. On 19th December 1915, he was appointed Commander-in-Chief in place of his old mentor, Sir John French. After the Armistice, he continued, until his death in 1928, to take a very active interest in the welfare of the soldiers who had won Britain's victory. Haig, never articulate at the best of times, found it hard to form close friendships or to project warmth in his relationships with his circle. History has not dealt kindly with this man, who carried perhaps the most awesome responsibility of any military leader in our history.

HAMILTON, General Sir Ian, 1853-1947

One of the breed of well-educated Victorian army officers who combined a passion for soldiering with literary and other interests. Born before the Crimean War, he belonged to the first intake of officers who owed their commissions to examination rather than purchase. Commissioned into the Gordon Highlanders, he distinguished himself in the Afghan War of 1879, and in 1885 published the first of many treaties on the art of war, in which he predicted that cavalry would have no role in the following century. He was the only senior commander in the South African War of 1899-1902 to achieve success in every task that he was required to perform.

In 1915, he was picked by Mr Winston Churchill to command the Gallipoli expedition. The force allocated to him was too small and too inexperienced, and soon became bogged down in the very sort of trench warfare that the operation was intended to break. Sir Ian Hamilton became the scapegoat for the inevitable disaster which followed, and spent the following two years facing a parliamentary enquiry, which finally exonerated him of all blame. He spent the postwar years devoting himself to the welfare of ex-servicemen.

HEAVY GUN

A gun of greater size, weight and range than a field gun. The lightest of these weapons could be dragged by teams of eight or more horses, or by steam traction engines. The biggest were either erected on static foundations or fired from railway mountings.

HOWITZER

A short barrelled gun designed to throw a heavy shell at high angle over a comparatively short range. Howitzers varied from light weapons that could be manhandled or carried by mules, to super-heavy weapons on railway mountings.

JOFFRE, Marshal Joseph Jacques Cesaire, 1852-1931

Of Spanish ancestry, Joseph Joffre was one of eleven children born to a village cooper in the Pyrenees. At the age of eighteen, he took part in the defence of Paris during the Franco-Prussian War, after which he was commissioned into the Corps of Engineers. His first duties involved the repair and strengthening of the Paris defences. However, the death of his young wife in 1884 so affected him that he applied for a posting to Indo-China where he spent three years as Chief Officer of the Engineers in Hanoi. In 1893, Joffre, now a major, commanded a column sent to restore order in Timbuktu. The operation, which involved an approach march through exceptionally difficult terrain of over 500 miles, was completely successful. In 1910, he was appointed to lead a contingency planning staff to formulate lines of communication plans which could be implemented should France go to war with Germany. The following year, Joffre, still aged only fifty nine, was promoted to Vice-President of the Higher Council and Chief of the General Staff. Under the French mobilisation plans, the holder of this office automatically assumed the appointment of Commander-in-Chief in time of war.

On 3rd August 1914, it was therefore General Joffre who took command of all French military forces in Europe. He was to provide the quiet, unshakeable leadership that held France together during the cataclysmic battles of 1914 and 1915. However, as a result of the degeneration of the situation in the Verdun sector and the failure of the French army on the Somme, coupled with an acrimonious clash of personalities, his authority was systematically stripped away until the title of Commander-in-Chief became merely a hollow sinecure, before the title itself was abolished in December 1916. Perhaps in compensation for his shabby treatment, Joffre was created a Marshal of France at the same time.

LORRAINE - See Alsace-Lorraine

LUDENDORF, Erich von, Field Marshal
Born 1865. A brilliant pre-war staff officer who oversaw the expansion of the German army in 1913 and was responsible for its mobilization plans the following year. Chief-of-Staff to General Hindenberg, who commanded the German 8th Army on the Eastern Front in 1915 during the period when the most crushing defeats (notably that of the Battle of Tannenberg) were inflicted on Russia. As Commander-in-Chief, von Ludendorf initiated the Spring offensive of 1918 - the final gamble which came so close to victory.

MARLBOROUGH, John Churchill, Field-Marshal, the Duke of 1650-1722
Commander-in-Chief of the united armies of England and Holland on the Continent during the War of Spanish Succession, 1702 to 1713.

MONTGOMERY, Bernard Law, Field-Marshal, Viscount 1887-1976
Commander-in-Chief 21 Army Group, North West Europe 1944-45.

MORTAR
A steel tube, closed at the bottom end, which was used to discharge a bomb by means of a propellant cartridge incorporated in the base of the bomb. Mortars had a very limited range and were fired at a high angle.

PALMERSTON, Henry John Temple, Viscount 1784-1865.
As British Foreign Minister, Palmerston was largely responsible for the establishment of Belgium as a neutral sovereign state in 1839.

PERSHING, General John Joseph 1860-1948

US soldier, born in very humble circumstances. Commissioned into the 6th US Cavalry in 1886 with whom he saw service against the Apache Indians that year, and against the Sioux in 1890. Appointed Military Attaché to Japan in 1905, his performance so impressed the President, Theodore Roosevelt, that he promoted him from Captain to Brigadier-General, therebye passing him over 862 senior officers! In 1916, Pershing commanded the expedition against Mexico. On the entry of United States into the Great War in April 1917, he was selected to command the US Expeditionary Force in France.

POSNAN

Also known as Poznan or Posen. This was one of the ancient Polish provinces annexed by Prussia in 1870 but returned to the re-established nation of Poland under the terms of the Treaty of Versailles in 1919.

RAWLINSON, General Sir Henry, Bt.

Born in 1864. Commissioned into the Coldstream Guards, Rawlinson was never a popular officer with his contemporaries, many of whom considered him 'too damned clever by half'. He took part in the Burma War, the Nile Expedition and the South African War, and, contrary to the custom of well-born young officers of that period, attended the Staff College. In 1902, he returned to command the Staff College. In 1914, Rawlinson went to France with the British Expeditionary Force, in command of the 3rd Division. Although possibly not a man gifted with undue imagination, he was capable of immensely painstaking and detailed work. His close analysis of the previous Great War battles led to a radical reappraisal of British tactics.

During the final Allied push launched on 8th August 1918, Rawlinson commanded the British 4th Army in a succession of spectacular victories which were to lead to the Armistice on 11th November. For this alone, he must be considered one of the great British generals of the war. He was raised to the peerage as Lord Rawlinson of Trent in 1919, and in that year was also given the unenviable task of extracting the Allied Russian Expeditionary Force from Archangel and Murmansk. He was appointed Commander-in-Chief India in 1920.

SAAR

An industrial and rich mining area on the Franco-German border north of Lorraine. Sovereignty of this area had been the subject of bitter disputes since the early 19th Century. In 1919, it became a protectorate of the League of Nations under the Treaty of Versailles, while at the same time its coal mines were ceded to France.

SCHLESWIG

A former Danish state, which lies between the Baltic and the North Sea, which was captured by Bismarck in 1863, and vested back to Denmark in 1919 under the Treaty of Versailles.

SCHLIEFFEN, Field Marshal Count Alfred von, 1833-1913

Prussian officer who served in the war against both Austria and France. He was appointed Chief of the General Staff in 1891, and from then until his retirement in 1907, formed and trained the most efficient military General Staff in Europe. Today, his main claim to fame rests in the so called 'Schlieffen Plan' for the conquest of France. This plan envisaged a wide outflanking movement through Belgium and Northern France, which would then sweep down to the south behind Paris. Thus, in one wide ranging operation, France would be cut off from any British aid and would be forced to fight an enemy in her rear. Schlieffen died in 1913, but in 1914 the German army executed a somewhat watered down version of his grand design. Had the German High Command had the courage to follow it more closely, the history of the Great War might have been very different.

STAFF COLLEGE

Originally founded in 1802 by the Duke of York as the Senior Department of the Royal Military College, it was intended to train officers in their professional duties, particularly as regards staff work. Sadly, the regimental system – in many ways the strength of the British Army – engendered an ethos which was hostile to the concept. Officers who sought entry to the Staff College were branded as being more interested in their own personal advancement than in the near sacred family of the regiment. Before 1914, many an extremely able officer served out his entire career in the same battalion. This not only produced an officer with a very limited military horizon, but created a serious shortage of trained staff officers to deal with the ever increasing demands of modern warfare.

STORM TROOPER

A German concept evolved in the early days of the war. Storm troopers were used to lead attacks. They were lightly equipped but carried large numbers of grenades, and sometimes did not carry any other weapon. They moved forward at great speed, sweeping aside minor opposition but attempting to bypass anything that appeared likely to hold them up. Storm troopers were not equipped to hold ground; this was done by conventional infantry who followed up as closely as possible.

TANK

The code name given to the British tracked armoured fighting vehicles to disguise their true function before they were used in battle in March 1916. Britain invented and built the first tanks in history. The appearance of these first machines was unique, being of rhomboidal form (an ideal shape to cross wide trenches). There were originally two types of tank, which looked very similar: the 'Male' was armed with a 6 pdr gun in each of the two sponsons which jutted out to either flank, and also had four machine guns; the 'Female' was fitted with five machine guns. Both types weighed 28 tons and had a maximum speed of about 4 mph.

Towards the end of the war a light tank, known as the 'Whippet', was brought into service. This, to modern eyes, was of a more conventional shape; it weighed 14 tons, was armed with three machine guns and could attain a maximum speed of 8 mph. 'Whippets' played their part in the final breakthrough before the Armistice, largely usurping the role of horsed cavalry.

The German answer to the tank was a square shaped vehicle. They were unpopular with their crews, who greatly preferred using captured British tanks. It is ironic that although Britain invented and first deployed tanks in battle, it was Germany who developed the weapon's potential in the years between the two World Wars.

TOWNSHEND, General Sir Charles 1861-1924

Commissioned into the Royal Marines, Townshend later transferred to the Indian Army. As a culmination of his varied and active military service, he was given command of the 6th Indian Division in Mesopotamia, with the task of advancing up the River Tigris to Baghdad. This operation was carried out with skill. However, he had outrun his 300 mile long line of communication and was forced to retire to a strong defensive position when within 25 miles of his objective. There, his Division, increasingly ravaged by disease, waited for the arrival of a relieving force. It never came. On 29th April 1916 General Townshend surrendered. Although probably over optimistic, General Townshend was carrying out the orders of his superior commander, and his Division was with an ace of achieving success. It is therefore tragic that this resourceful and highly professional senior officer should have been branded as the man responsible for the greatest British surrender since Yorktown in 1781.

TREATIES OF PARIS, 1814 and 1815

The first treaty of Paris was convened by the Allies following the initial abdication of Napoleon Bonaparte in 1814. It was designed to restore Louis XVIII to the throne of France and to establish a lasting peace in Europe. The treaty was signed by Britain, Austria, Russia and Prussia on 11th April 1814. The second treaty of Paris was convened as a result of Napoleon's escape from Elba and subsequent defeat at Waterloo in June 1815. Both Treaties were finally ratified at the Congress of Vienna.

WELLINGTON, Arthur Wellesley, Field-Marshal, the Duke of 1769-1852

Wellington, having first served in India, became known as 'The Iron Duke'. He was Commander-in-Chief of the British Army in Spain, Portugal and France from 1809-1818. Prime Minister of Britain 1828-1830.

WILHELM II, Kaiser, 1859-1941

Son of Prince Frederich of Prussia and Princess Victoria who was a daughter of Queen Victoria. Not until he succeeded his father at the age of sixty, was he allowed any real authority. He drifted from university to the army. Sustained work was never demanded of him, and consequently he never learnt to do any. Arrogant and superficially intelligent, he was capable of making quick decisions without thinking through any long term effects. Never doubting his divine right as monarch, he believed that God alone could direct decisions. This attitude soon made it impossible for him to work with his highly experienced Chancellor, Prince Otton von Bismarck, who was summarily dismissed on 18th March 1890. Thus Germany was left in the hands of a man who could not lay down a consistent line of policy, for the simple reason that he possessed no solid views. The absence of any firm leadership, in the most powerful nation in Europe during the late 19th and early 20th Centuries, was undoubtedly one of the factors that led to the Great War.

WILSON, General Sir Henry (later Field Marshall) 1864-1922

Born and brought up in Ireland, Wilson was commissioned into the Rifle Brigade in 1884. He saw active service in the Burma War of 1886 and the South African War of 1899. During the first years of the 20th century, he worked with the committee tasked with the reappraisal of British Army organisation and tactics, which had proved so inadequate in South Africa. As Commandant of the Staff College in 1906, he projected a deep impression on many young officers who were to play a major role in the forthcoming war. He foresaw the advent of the European conflict and threw his weight behind the formulation of contingency plans to meet this eventuality. In particular, he forged close links with the French Staff College, emphasising the need for common staff and tactical procedures. The Commandant of the French Staff College, Colonel Foch (later the French Commander-in-Chief) became a firm friend.

On mobilisation in 1914 he accompanied the British Expeditionary Force to France, as the Deputy Chief of Staff. Wilson's knowledge of the French Army, and his close friendship with many influential French officers, was of inestimable value, particularly at a time when the British Commander-in-Chief, Sir John French, made no secret of his disdain of all things French. Wilson was essentially a staff officer with a highly developed gift of intuition. He was also highly articulate and thus capable of expressing complex ideas with great clarity.

In 1920 Wilson was appointed Chief of the Imperial General Staff, but as an Irishman with a warm love of Ireland, found his loyalties badly torn. Following his retirement in 1922, he entered Parliament where he became one of the most outspoken critics of British policy in Ireland. On 31st May, in his last speech to the Commons, he concluded:

"I wonder when the moment will come when the Government will have the honesty and truthfulness to say, 'we have miscalculated every single element in the Irish problem. We are exceedingly sorry for all the terrible things that have happened owing to our actions. We beg leave to return to private life and never to appear again'".

Three weeks later he was murdered by Irish terrorists on the front steps of his house. So died an Irish patriot.

WILSON, Thomas Woodrow, 1856-1924

Born of Irish/Scots ancestry, he became the 28th President of the USA in 1913. Wilson initially proclaimed a policy of strict non-involvement in the Great War. It was only after German submarine attacks were reported as being made on US shipping that Wilson reluctantly entered the war on 6th April 1917.

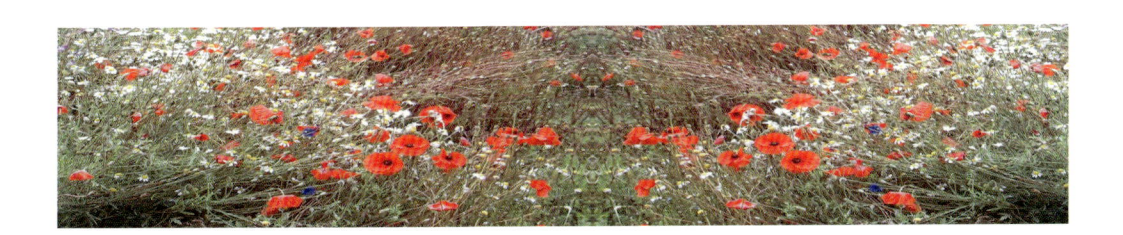

Bibliography

Although it is usual to provide a list of books and references, the history of the First World War has generated so enormous a volume of literature that I felt it futile to provide a full bibliography of books on the period, such a list being considered beyond the scope and intention of this work. However, the following list includes some of the more important books on the First World War, especially those on the military campaigns of the period.

Title	Author	Publisher
Beneath Flanders' Fields	Peter Barton, Peter Doyle & Johan Vanderwalle	Spellmount Publishers Ltd
Kitchener. Architect of Victory	George Cassau	Kimber
Dardanelles Dilemma	Keble Chatterton	Rich & Cowan Ltd
The British Campaigns in Europe	Arthur Conan Doyle	Geoffrey Bles
1914	Field Marshal Lord French	Constable
The Little Field Marshall	Richard Holmes	Weidenfeld & Nicholson
Somme	Lyn MacDonald	Penguin Books
The Battle of Ypres, 1915	J McWilliams & R J Steele	Vanwell Publishing Ltd
Gallipoli	Alan Moorehead	Wordsworth
Ypres, 1914	Otto Schwink	Constable
The First World War	Hew Strachan	Oxford University Press
Douglas Haig. The Educated Soldier	John Terraine	Leo Cooper
Mons	John Terraine	Batsford
Military Operations, 1914	War Office	Battery Press
Great War, 1916	War Office	Shearer
The Mesopotamia Campaign (7 Vols)	War Office	HMSO
Military Operations in Egypt & Palestine (6 Vols)	War Office	HMSO
1918 Military Operations, France & Belgium	War Office	Naval & Military Press
Passchendaele	Philip Warner	Sidgwick & Jackson

Hugo White

The son of an officer in the 7th Gurkha Rifles, Hugo White was brought up in India, until sent to board in England at the age of 7. After education at Wellington College, he enlisted in the Coldstream Guards. Following Sandhurst, he was commisssioned in the Somerset Light Infantry. A wide range of military experience encompassed Germany, Cyprus, Gibralter, Libya, two years with the Parachute regiment which included an emergency tour in Jordan, Malaysia during the insurgency and for ten years after independence, not to mention two years in the strike carrier 'Eagle' as one of two 'pongoes' amongst 250 naval officers. Other service included roles in Northern Ireland with the Ulster Defence Regiment, a period with the Light Infantry at Shrewsbury and a further period seconded to the Royal Ulster Constabulary Special Branch in Northern Ireland.

After some forty years of service, Hugo White retired to assist in reorganising the regimental museum in Bodmin, then becoming Regimental Secretary of the Duke of Cornwall's Light Infantry.

Always interested in military history he has made this subject a life long study. His books include *One and All*, the encyclopedic history of the Duke of Cornwall's Light Infantry from 1702 to 1959, which includes analysis of every campaign, including many little known wars and actions. Married, with two children and four grandchildren, he now lives in Padstow, where he enjoys rowing Cornish pilot gigs, continues to research military history, and keeps a succession of lurchers.

His works of military history remain unique in the depth and extent of the research and in being the product of an author who understands not just the subject but the actions and life of a soldier.

One and All:
A History of the Duke of Cornwall's Light Infantry, 1702-1959

ISBN 1 873951 45 0

Hugo White has also written a masterly account of war, of peace and of little known campaigns fought in many countries around the world.

The book has 594 pages, copious illustrations and many maps.
The paperback version is available at £16.95, plus £3.50 p&p in UK.
Tabb House, 01841 532316

It has 'Definitive history …'   *Richard Holmes*

'Information conveyed in extremely readable, even moving prose. As a lover of books, I am relishing it.'   *Christine San José*

'This magnificent chronicle.'   *Professor Charles Thomas*

'While I was reading it, I found myself wanting this big book to be longer, so that I could have more of it.'   *Giles Clotworthy*

'A masterpiece.'   *Western Morning News*

'Highly readable, well-structured and well-researched, with a narrative that proceeds at a Light Infantry [fast] pace.'   *Major General A. Makepeace-Warne,*
MBE (KOYLI & Light Infantry)

'Captures both the broad sweep of history that is the essential backdrop to regimental history and the details of the DCLI's doings in war and peace. Written by an author of insight and understanding.'
General Sir Richard Trant,
KCB, DSc, DL (Royal Artillery)

Pasticcio, publishers

Recent publications

Thomas Wood Holgate by Stephen Tyrrell
Thomas Wood Holgate (1869-1954) exhibited in London before 1914 and in London and Cornwall thereafter. This book provides a list of his recorded work and the background needed for assessment of his artistic achievement.
Full colour 72 illustrations

Trewinnard: A Cornish History by Stephen Tyrrell; introduction by Sir John Nott
This book covers not just the history of Trewinnard and its owning families but is also an introduction to the history of south west Cornwall.
Reissued in soft back with 224 pages and over 370 illustrations

Coins and Travels in Greece by Harold Mattingly; drawings by Joanna Mattingly
Many books record the coins of the ancient world, but few prove so entertaining an introduction to the coins of Greece as this volume. This is an enjoyable and charmingly illustrated short introduction to study of the period.
Softback in full colour with 232 illustrations

Caerhays Castle   by Charles Williams, Peter Herring, Stephen Tyrrell et al; edited Stephen Tyrrell
This substantial book has been reviewed as the exemplar of country house histories. It covers not only the romantic castle, historic estate and owning families but also the early history of the area and the important gardens.
Hardbound; full colour; approximately 630 illustrations

A Visitor in Cornwall   by Stephen Tyrrell; watercolour illustrations by Joanna Mattingly.
Delightful watercolour sketches of historic Cornish properties with notes on 70 buildings, several pages of anecdotes, and even a recipe or two. Winner of annual award for best illustrated book in Cornwall.
Softback; full colour; 94 illustrations

Books now in preparation include:

The Royal Cornwall Yacht Club   By Andrew Pool Publication Autumn 2014

The Roman Occupation of Cornwall   By Stephen Tyrrell Publication July 2014

Boconnoc: A Medieval & Georgian family house   Publication: Spring 2015

Early Decorative Plasterwork: The Decorative Plasterwork of Cornwall 1550-1670
An introduction to the development of the Cornish house and a gazetteer, history and commentary on Cornish houses and interiors from small farmhouses to great houses. Two volumes: Publication: Late 2015

Pasticcio is always interested in considering new works for publication.
Details, contents and sample pages from Pasticcio books can be seen on
www.pasticcio.co.uk.
Books can be ordered from the office on 01326 340153

Pasticcio